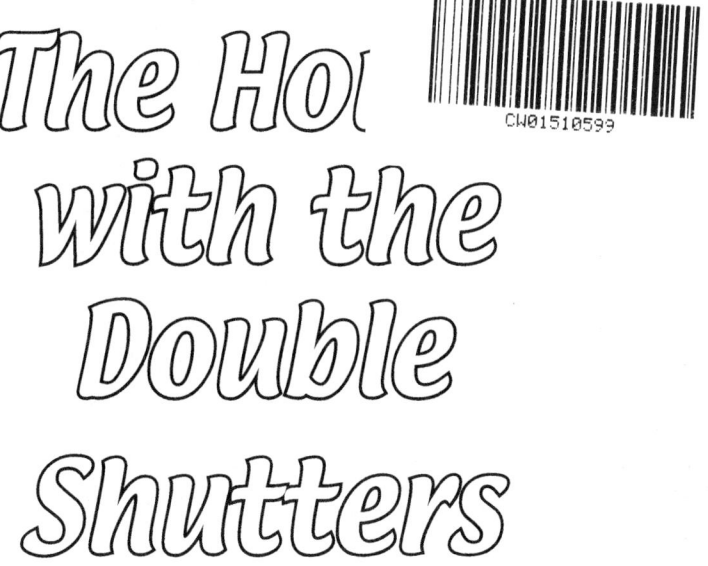

The Hou
with the
Double
Shutters

In search of my
Dutch family's history

Wim Zwalf

CW01510599

The House with the Double Shutters

First published in Great Britain in 2024
This edition, January 2025

Copyright – Wim Zwalf

Wim Zwalf has asserted his right under the Copyright, Designs and
Patents Act 1988 to be identified as the author of this work.
All rights reserved. No part of this publication may be reproduced,
distributed, or transmitted in any form or by any means, including
photocopying, recording, or other electronic or mechanical methods,
without the prior written permission of the author.

ISBN: 978-1-7392267-2-5

Pictures:
Unless stated, pictures are from the author's collection.
Thank you to all other suppliers of pictures. Every effort has been
made to acknowledge the source of specific illustrations and
photographers where they are known and to ensure copyright
has not been infringed. We apologise if you believe your work
has been used without permission. If this is the case, contact the
publisher in the first instance.

steve@stevepennymedia.co.uk
A Penny For Your Sports Publications production
https://tinyurl.com/spennymedia

Contents

*For Louis and Johanna's great-grandchildren
and Joop and Patricia's grandchildren*

*Luke, Hannah, Leah, Tristan, Sebastian,
Liesbeth and Oliver*

'Ut non obliviscar'

*And in loving memory of Louis' grandson
Christopher Zwalf, 1949-2021*

Zij die zich aan de vijand verkochten

Hun rest slechts schande en schaamte

Het rad van historie wentelt verder

Wat boven is komt onder

Wat onder is komt boven

Radio Herrijzend Nederland 1945

Those who sold themselves to the enemy

For them only scandal and shame remain

The wheel of history turns further

What is above comes underneath

What is underneath comes to the top

Radio Netherlands Resurgent 1945

The House with the Double Shutters

Introduction

It all started some 60 years ago when I was a student at King's College, London. I was walking along Hatton Gardens (the jewellery quarter of London), and saw a sign over a shop 'Zwalf and Mellek, diamond merchants'.

Never having come across anyone else with the surname Zwalf before, I went in and asked for Mr Zwalf. Herman Zwalf appeared from the back and we tried to work out how we were connected, as we both had Dutch fathers. However, we came to no conclusion.

I asked my father if he knew how we were connected and he too drew a blank. This triggered my interest in the family and the family history that I have compiled over the past 30 years-or-so and this is the result.

The information has come from many sources. I was given a great deal of help by Jane Borst, whose family hid my grandmother during the Second World War. She did a lot of research for me in the 1980s. Fellow family historians also gave me advice or helped me find the right bits of information and a number of archivists in various locations managed to find some of the things that I was looking for.

The internet has, of course, greatly assisted in research, as has the interest that has developed in the Netherlands into the events of the Second World War and the fate of the Jews in particular. In this regard the Amsterdam Municipal Archives and the Netherlands Institute for War Documentation and Holocaust Studies have been most approachable and very helpful, both with advice, clarification and documents.

My father Joseph, who was always known as 'Joop', never spoke of relatives in the Netherlands and only told us of snippets about his childhood and his time as a student. My grandmother, Johanna Zwalf-Pampel, did occasionally talk of "my husband" (she always referred to Louis as such), especially when I used to visit her in Amsterdam, when I was at school in The Hague.

I would spend the day, normally a Saturday, with her in Amsterdam. She would meet me at the Central Station and we would go and have coffee with her friends, a group of old ladies who met every Saturday in a posh cafe not far from the station.

There I would be fawned over by these ladies, who mixed their Dutch with another language that I did not understand, but which I now guess was Yiddish.

We would then go to the cinema, or the zoo, or the Rijksmuseum, then to her flat and have a meal with her sister, Tante Fre. Occasionally she would then talk about the pre-war years, Joop growing up, and the events of the war. She also sometimes told me bits of family history that she knew.

My grandmother's wartime:

I have gathered this story from a variety of sources. Some of it was told to me by my grandmother and I have both met and corresponded with some of those who hid my grandmother during the Second World War.

I have also had lots of help from Jane Borst and Trudi Bos (a retired chief librarian who wrote *Op Zoek naar een plaats om thuis te komen* [Searching for a Place to Call Home] the history of the Jewish inhabitants of Velsen, where my father grew up) as well as correspondence in the early part of this century with Christa Poel, another whose family hid my grandmother.

Trudi in particular has helped with the background of the family's life in Velsen and she has generously allowed me to use her research, for which I am very grateful. There are a number of things I would never have found out without her help.

Joop's escape to England:

I have always had in mind an event that happened in 1958. I was about 11 years old and we were living at No.99 Johan van Oldenbarneveltlaan, in The Hague. My father met up with an old school friend, Henk Stol, whom he had not seen since the Second World War. I think Henk lived in Suriname and was on leave in Holland. Joop said that if I sat quietly in the corner I could listen.

Some of this story comes from a variety of books that have been published over the years and which detail some of the story of Joop's escape from German-occupied Holland. The three books that give details of the escape vary somewhat in detail, so I have put it together with what I heard Joop tell. The books are *The Schakel* [The Link] by Frank Visser, *Tulpen voor Wilhemina* [Tulips for Wilhemina] by Agnes Dessing, and *Vrijheid achter de Horizon* [Freedom over the Horizon] by Jan Bruin and Jan van der Werff.

Joop himself kept his background and his wartime experiences behind a thick wall of silence. I suspect that to his dying day it was too painful. There is no doubt that those who suffered so much have the absolute right to keep the details of their past to themselves.

Only once did Joop allude to his past and heritage and told my younger brother Chris and me: "If you don't know, then what happened to me and my family won't happen to you". It was most definitely not a subject that could be raised or discussed! Similarly my grandmother was always reluctant to divulge the horrors and persecution she suffered, perhaps out of fear of creating despair in her grandchildren.

She however was much more forthcoming than her son, and did from time to time tell me stories of our family but it was always "they died in the war" with no further details.

When I was a boy in Holland the plight of the Jews during the war was just not spoken about. However, I believe that those who survived the Holocaust, and those who helped and sheltered them, putting their own safety and the safety of their families at risk, need their courage to be told and remembered.

ivil registration started in Holland in 1811, one of the reforms that Napoleon introduced. Before 1811 there were no Zwalfs in the *'Schout en Schepenen'* registers in Amsterdam. These are the pre-civil registration registers. But the following names do appear:

Swalb, Swalef, Zwalff, Swaleff, Swalve, Swallow, Zwaalf, Swalp, Zwaelp, Swelp, Zwaluff, Swalleft.

Clearly the Zwalf family (or more like a clan) was well established in Amsterdam at that time. Spelling was a moveable feast in the 18th Century. Before that, in the 17th Century, Rembrandt spelled his own name in a variety of ways when signing his paintings. In addition to the variableness of spelling, it is perhaps unlikely that any Zwalfs could actually write anyway. They may have spoken Dutch and Yiddish and had a smattering of Hebrew, which they may have been able to write, but probably not written Dutch.

When Joseph Moses Swalef registered his son in 1816 it was misheard and registered as 'Zwalf'. But now it is written in stone, officially registered, and no civil servant worth their salt is going to change it. All those with the surname spelled as Zwalf are therefore descendants of Hartog Joseph Zwalf. All Joseph Moses Swalf's other children are registered as Swalf or Swalef.

The pre-1811 registers are incomplete, some of the synagogue records went missing during World War Two, and so there is only incomplete evidence before then. However, Salomon Moses Swalb, aged 34, son of Moses Juda Levy, deceased, and Sara Joseph, married Rebecca Abraham Cohen, aged 34 on June 16, 1814. They already had children – Moses Salomon, Abraham, and Lea. I believe that this Salomon Moses Swalb is a brother of Joseph Moses Swalef.

The 'Moses' indicated their father's name, (the patronymic) and his children have very characteristic Zwalf first names. In addition they both have as their mother Sarah Joseph. So Joseph's father was Moses, his grandfather Juda, and his great-grandfather

Levy. All these names appear with regularity among later Zwalfs. So Levy would have been born around 1690.

All this conjecture is strengthened by the fact that Joseph Moses Swallow is the name given at his death in the Israel Hospital at the age of 77. Incidentally the two witnesses to the death could not write their names in the register because it was the Sabbath!

He must have died on Friday, April 27, 1849, registered the following day. He is described as born in Amsterdam in 1772. So we can suppose that Moses Juda Zwalf was born about 1745; Juda Levy Zwalf about 1720; and Levy Zwalf 1690, or thereabouts. It appears that there were Swalefs (and various spellings) in Amsterdam from about 1625.

T he impression that one gains from the largish Zwalf family in Amsterdam is that they were already well settled there from before the middle of the 17th Century. Amsterdam was the flourishing centre of the States General of the Netherlands, where culture, commerce, banking, and invention were thriving.

Not only was this the case but the atmosphere of tolerance and freedom was palpable. Persecuted Jews from all over Europe settled there. Between 1635 and 1670, 252 Ashkenazi Jews married, of these 177 came from Germany, Austria, Bohemia and Lorraine, 28 from Poland and Lithuania and 35 were already born in Holland. (See 'Memorboek' – a 1,000-plus-page volume about the Jews in the Netherlands)

It is likely then that the Zwalf clan were already long-time residents by the time we first hear of them. So they could well have come from the East, but...

Jane Borst, who did a lot of work for me in the Amsterdam Archives, contacted a Harry Swalef, who lives in Belgium. In correspondence in 1984 he wrote:

> "I am by profession a linguist and so have been very interested in the origins of the word 'Swalef' and all its variants including Zwalf and Swallow. I started by seeing if the word 'swalef' appeared in any European language. It does not. An acquaintance stumbled by chance, while reading a book on Jewish culture and art, upon the fact that the word is of Arabic origin.
>
> "In Arabic the word 'swalef' has a number of closely related meanings. The stem of the word is 's l f' and the plural noun is 'swalf' or 'swalef'. Now among the Jews living in North Africa and the Middle East a language developed that was based in Arabic (Judeo-Arabic) comparable to the Eastern language based on Judeo- German, Yiddish. In this mixed language, Judeo-Arabic, many Arab words developed specific Jewish meanings.

Among non-Jews in the Middle East, 'swalef' (or 'sawalif'
or 'swalif') meant the 'hair in front of the ears on the temples'
(i.e. sideburns). In the Middle East it became among Jews the
expression for 'payes or payot' the curling locks of hair worn by
orthodox Jews.

"In the Arabic of North Africa 'swalef' (especially Morocco)
it meant the long plaits worn by women. The Moroccan Jewish
women did wear until the 1940s a big wig, which was worn
at festivals and especially at weddings, when they would be
wonderfully decorated. Both the wig (made of horse or cow
hair, usually the tail, human hair was strictly forbidden) and
the decoration were called 'swalef'. Moroccan Jews have told me
that their grandmothers indeed wore 'swalef'. I have a number
of books with illustrations of these 'swalef-wigs'"

However, my DNA results indicate that my Y chromosomes are 48% Ashkenazi, so perhaps the suggestion that we are of Sephardic descent is unlikely. Although the fact that Hartog Joseph Zwalf married Lea Castro, who was of Sephardic descent, and whose grandparents were born in Livorno, Italy, and great-grandparents born in Portugal, may indicate that there was a Sephardic element to the Zwalfs.

There are registered marriages of Zwalfs with people with the surnames of Castro, Allegro, Querido and Murpurgo, which seems to indicate a Sephardic connection. The majority of Zwalf marriages though are Ashkenazi.

Joseph Hartog Zwalf (1841-1910) was the eldest of eight children of Hartog Joseph Zwalf (1814-1889), a tailor, and Lea Abraham Castro (1816-1881). Hartog must have been reasonably well off as he is listed as travelling to London in July 1851 and spending some time there.

His son Joseph was firstly married to Eva Godefroi, with whom he had seven children, of whom only two survived childhood, Lea and Klara. After Eva's death, Joseph married his next-door neighbour, a widow Hanna Carels, (1855-1936) the widow of Abraham Salomans, a diamond polisher, who had five children, of whom only two survived childhood, Grietje and Marianne (Tante Marianne), and then together they had two children Levie and Hartog Naphtalie.

My grandmother used to tell me that Hanna would tell Joseph: "Do something about it, your children and my children are fighting with our children!"

Joseph was an entrepreneur who had a finger in all sorts of pies. In 1872 he was a cigar dealer in London, where he lived in Raven Row, the street next to the Royal London Hospital in the East End (where my eldest two children, Luke and Hannah, were born just over a century later) and where a child 'Moses' died of 'convulsions' at the age of 14 months. Joseph also visited the United States at some stage, but by the 1890s he was back in Amsterdam, living on the Rapenburg.

In 1890 he was listed as secretary of a friendly society established for diamond workers. In 1895 he was listed with M Citroen (his brother-in-law) as the proprietor of a hotel, which had been established for an international exhibition. In 1887 he was an agent for *kosher pesach brood* [kosher passover bread – an unleavened flatbread or cracker] but by 1889 he was the manufacturer of the 'Champion' gas mantles.

This business seems to have thrived, despite an 1899 fire, and remained in the family until the 1930s. When electricity first started to be introduced in Amsterdam, Joseph was alleged to have said: "It will never catch on!"

An advert for Joseph Zwalf's factory:
It translates as: 'Gas mantle factory 'The Crown',
Rapenburgplein 3, Amsterdam, owner J. Zwalf,
is the only and cheapest address where one can get the soft burning
mantles at 8 cents apiece (to say EIGHT Cents)
All own manufactured and not second hand.
Ready for immediate lighting'

This is a translation of an article in the newspaper of April 20, 1899 detailing the events of the day:

Fire at Rapenburg

This morning at 11 o'clock Mr Zwalf was in his shop at Rapenburg 99 making gas mantles. He was using a beaker with a mixture of ether of sulphur and other chemicals with an open gas flame, all of which he had left next to each other, while he had to leave it for a moment.

Suddenly he heard an explosion and noticed that flames were emanating from his workbench. He had time to grab his five year old son, who was in the back room, and fled to the safety of the street.

The flames took substantial hold before the fire brigade could get there and the shop, the room above and the two back rooms were aflame. With two fire engines under the command of fire superintendent Proost the flames were brought under control.

Four rooms were completely burned out, while the residents upstairs suffered some smoke and fire damage. Everything was insured. The upstairs was occupied by Mr G Meenhow, a carpenter.

Another local paper stated:

The fire brigade was immediately warned and with the help of two hoses in the canal, the fire was soon extinguished and limited to the ground floor. The shop, and the workshop behind, was completely burned out. Upstairs some windows were blown out and curtains singed. The house opposite had the paintwork peeled off the woodwork from the flames that shot out.

Joseph Hartog seems to have been quite prosperous as the family was settled in Amsterdam and he eventually retired to Wormen, near Apeldoorn, before his death at the age of 69. The business was passed to a nephew until it was declared bankrupt in the 1930s, by which time most of Amsterdam was supplied with electricity, after obviously 'catching on' despite Joseph's earlier comment.

Levie Zwalf was born in Amsterdam on March 17, 1889 and was always known as Louis. He was the eldest son of Joseph Zwalf's second marriage, to the widow Hannah Carels. Nearly three years later another son was born, Hartog Naphtalie (always known as Hendrik).

Their upbringing was typical of Dutch-Jewish families in a Jewish part of Amsterdam. They both had further education and qualified, Louis as an electrician and Hendrik as a chemist.

Louis, standing right, during his National Military Service.

Like all young men, Louis was conscripted and did his military service. He would have been 18, the normal time to do military service in 1907. During the First World War, in 1916 he was called up again, but as the Netherlands was a neutral country, he only served in a reserved capacity.

He met Johanna Pampel and they married in Zandam in 1917. Although they both lived in Amsterdam, like many Amsterdam Jews, they chose to marry in Zaandam as it was very much cheaper there! Johanna, just as Louis, came from a Jewish family who had, like the Zwalfs, been living in Amsterdam since the 18th Century. Her great-great grandfather Isaac Pampel was born in Amsterdam in 1735.

Louis and Johanna's 1917 engagement photographs.

The following September (1918) their son Joseph was born at Pieter Aertstraat 26, Amsterdam. Joseph was always known as Joop. We have to assume that their life was pretty much unremarkable and that they were a typical assimilated Dutch Jewish family. How close they were to the Jewish community is not known, but certainly Joop was circumcised in the traditional manner.

In 1924 Louis' younger brother Hendrik moved to Velsen on the North Sea coast, where he got a job as a chemist in the laboratory of the Van Gelder paper factory. He and his wife Jetta Barnstein (Tante Jet) and their little daughter Hanna lived in the Melklaan. In 1927 Louis, Johanna and Joop also moved to Velsen, also in *Melklaan* (Milk Lane, a street in the north of the municipality), as Louis got a position as an electrician at the *Hoogovens* [blast furnaces], which was then the largest iron and steel foundry in the Netherlands. He was one of the few permanent employees. In the 1930s it was the firm's policy to employ as few workers permanently as possible, as there was a great number of unemployed people, not least because of the virtually total standstill of the fishing industry. Every day hundreds of men would queue in the hope of a day's work.

By 1914 Louis was already a member of the Nederlandsche

Metaalbewerkers Bond, the Dutch metal workers trade union and once employed at the steel works was active in the trade union there and was secretary of the local branch of the Metalworkers' Union.

Hoogovens: Haven, Transporteurs en Hitsers   IJMUIDEN

Hoogovens steel works in 1926.   *(Picture: North Holland's Archives)*

The background to the union representation at the Hoogovens:

Louis is mentioned in the 1930s in newspaper reports of the annual meeting of the Metal Workers Union. In 1932 he is a delegate at the national congress. He was then a candidate for the national board of the union but lost out to a fellow unionist from the same steel works.

He also asked critical questions of the leadership of the union. He asked the union if they had in fact done their utmost to avoid the lowering of the wages of the workers at the steel plant by 5%. He said that it appeared they had not and that it simply 'showed the impotence of the union'. The senior officers of the union replied that 'we all must strive to have a proper perspective, we cannot fight everything and we have to take into account the current situation'.

Louis, with other delegates, demanded to know that in this time of crisis, unemployment and poverty if it was right for the union's management to increase their own salaries. However, the majority of the delegates decided that it was not appropriate nor in the interest of the working classes to discuss this in public as it would only play into the hands of their class enemies!

At the congress in 1934 the union management of the ANMB were allergic to the criticism and Louis and others were labelled as agitators on the radical left. According to the newspaper *Het Volk* this did not prevent Louis from raising a critical tone. In the article Louis claimed that the leader of the steelworks branch of the union, Rijk de Waal, was not even vaguely militant.

Instead of a speech to galvanise the workers De Waal advised them to accept the lowering of their wages, which the directors of the steelworks had proposed. He should, Louis declared, have given the workers 'a belt under their heart' but instead the union had 'taken the oomph out of the workers'.

Louis still wasn't finished. He was critical of the high cost of the personnel of the union's administration and the outlay for the congress. In addition the high cost of producing the newspaper *The Metalworker* was as far as he was concerned 'not proportional with the contents of the paper or the interest that people have for it'.

According to the newspaper Mr Houben, who was both editor and chief executive, reacted as if stung by a wasp. According to him Louis had no real criticism of the contents but could only stab him in the back and 'that clearly betrays the kind of person he was'. Houben added that Zwalf would probably been less critical if the paper 'glorified Communism more'. Louis protested against this attempt at this 'polemic', but the chairman did give him a telling off. He distanced himself from Louis' inappropriate remarks, which were personal opinions and not those of the IJmuiden section.

The IJmuiden delegates did in fact back up the head office management. So Louis obviously had Communist sympathies but it is doubtful that he was unfamiliar with the opinions of his own department in IJmuiden.

My grandmother always said that the three things that Louis despised most were the three Ks [in Dutch: *de Kroeg, de Kerk en de Kazerne*] the pub, the church and the barracks. He was a member of the *Sociaal Democratiesche Arbeiders Partij* [the Social Democratic Workers Party]. The SDAP was founded in 1894 with left wing views, striving for a socialist society where the means of production were in the hands of the state, but by the 1920s its programme was more central and in the coalition Government of 1939 it provided two ministers. It was banned by the German occupiers and resurrected in 1946, with other parties, as the *Partij van de Arbeid*, the Dutch Labour Party.

Vote Red, choose candidates of the Social Democratic Workers Party.

Louis was a member of the SDAP, and not the Communists. I was always told that he was a Communist by my father's cousin, who obviously got it wrong, but he was clearly of a left-wing political persuasion.

There was a lot of criticism of the movement in the 1930s and it is possible that he joined the *Onafhankelijke Socialisische Partij* [the Independent Socialist Party] a left-wing splinter party of people who had left the SDAP, as many in IJmuiden did.

Melklaan in about 1930.   *(Picture: Beeldbank Historische Kring Velsen)*

Joop used to tell how when they moved to Velsen, their first house, in the Melklaan, did not have running water, and that his first job in the morning was to go to the yard and pump water for the family.

The family had moved to the Zeeweg in Velsen Zuid by 1933. Some of Joop's primary schooling must have been there, but certainly his secondary education was at the RHBS [Rijks Hogere Burgers School, the National Higher Citizens School], which was within walking distance and was known as the *Groene Kikkerschool* [the Green Frog School], because the roof tiles were green.

At some stage in his teens Joop went on an educational cruise to Norway, which I think was organised by one of the trade unions. He also visited his cousin, Lydia, in Aalborg, Denmark, where his uncle Hartog (Johanna's brother) had a tobacco business. Although he rarely spoke of pre-Second World War events, he did tell of his closeness to his father and how on one occasion they went strawberry picking together and ate so many that he could not stand them for many years! He was also a keen hockey player and was a member of the 'Strawberries' the hockey club in Driehuis.

The Rijks Hogere Burgers, Groene Kikkerschool.

(Picture: Beeldbank Historische Kring Beverwijk)

Joop's passport, issued when he was 17 for his trip to Denmark to visit his Uncle Hartog (Johanna's brother), his wife Elsa and cousin Lydia.

A school football team residential in August 1929. Joop is in the middle row, standing right.

Johanna, Louis and Joop, above, pictured on September 1, 1932.

Right, Joop and his cousin Leni de Zoete.

At 19 Joop passed his matriculation RHBS [*Rijks Hogere Burgers School* – National Higher Citizens School] with an A grade and moved to Rotterdam, where he went into digs. He had been turned down for compulsory military service in 1938 due to his poor eyesight. After having passed accountancy exams, he took up a position with a firm of accountants in Rotterdam. Joop was a junior trainee with the firm of Moret & Stark and was taking courses at the Netherlands School of Economics in Rotterdam (now Erasmus University) in economics and administration in the evenings. While he was living in Rotterdam the Germans invaded the Netherlands on May 10, 1940 and Rotterdam was bombed to destruction on May 14.

Rotterdam destroyed.   *(Picture: National Maritime Museum)*

Fortuitously, Joop was back home in Velsen for the long weekend (Whitsun) because he had a hockey match, which due to the invasion had been postponed.

In September 1940 he was still, as normal, playing in the Strawberries first team and was still in the team the following Easter. From October 1941 the Germans forbade Jews from being members of non-Jewish clubs and associations. This must have been a wake-up call for Joop and his family.

Already by January 1941, Louis, Johanna and Joop had registered in the Velsen Municipality as 'People of Jewish blood' as required by the occupying German powers. In the meantime Louis could continue working in the steel works because he was in a protected occupation and did not have to move to Amsterdam as most of the Jewish inhabitants of Velsen had been forced to do under a German order.

Louis must have been aware of the fact that Dutch Jews were being forced into isolation. It was about this time that Louis became involved in illegal work by helping to find addresses where Jewish children could be safely 'adopted' by Christian families.

The Netherlands had been a neutral country for generations and the Dutch Government thought that even after the *Anschluss* of Austria and Czechoslovakia and the invasion of Poland in 1939, that they would remain impartial.

The Dutch army was rather old fashioned and ill equipped. After all, the last invasion of the Netherlands was under Napoleon in 1811. But on May 10, 1940 the German army invaded the Netherlands. Rotterdam was heavily bombed, with about 800 people killed and 25,000 homes destroyed. On May 15 the Dutch army, outnumbered and ill equipped, surrendered. The Queen, Wilhelmina, and Dutch Cabinet had escaped to England, as had the Dutch Navy and much of the merchant marine.

Immediately following the German occupation, anti-Semitic measures were implemented. Between September and November 1940, Jewish newspapers were closed down, Jewish civil servants were sacked and the assets of all Jewish businesses were registered. Following this, Jewish students were also expelled from schools and universities. Jews were no longer allowed to participate in sport.

In January 1941, all Jews living within the Netherlands were ordered to register with the *Schutzstaffel* (SS). A total of 159,806 people registered, including 19,561 born of mixed marriages. The total also included about 25,000 Jewish refugees from Germany.

During the winter of 1940/41 members of the Dutch Nazis, the NSB [*Nationaal-Socialistische Beweging*, National Socialist Movement in the Netherlands] harassed Jews in Amsterdam's Jewish quarter. They humiliated the residents and stole their belongings. However, some of them resisted and formed 'thug' groups. They were supported in their resistance by other non-Jewish people in Amsterdam.

The Dutch Nazis tried to persuade reluctant café owners to put up signs with texts such as 'Forbidden for Jews' or 'Jews not welcome'. This led to several riots in the vicinity of the Rembrandtplein – one of the busiest squares in the city.

On February 9, 1941, members of the NSB, protected by German soldiers, forced their way into the Alcazar café, because Jewish artists were still performing there. This led to a brawl in which 23 people were injured. In the early evening of February 11, a group of marching and singing NSB members went to beat up Jews. A Communist gang was alerted and came to the aid of the Jews. After the fight, which lasted only a few minutes, Hendrik Koot (one of the NSB members) appeared to have lost consciousness. The police found his body and he died on February 14 1941 without regaining consciousness.

In the unrest that arose around the riots and Koot's death, the German occupying forces held major raids in the Jewish quarter on February 22 and 23, 1941. On the orders of Heinrich Himmler, 427 Jewish men between the ages of 20 and 35 were arrested and brought together in Jonas Daniël Meijerplein.

It gave fuel to join the ensuing February strike en masse, which was shortly put down by the occupiers.

The raid on Jews in February 1941 at the Jonas Daniël Meijerplein. One of the young men was Joop's cousin Moses Leyden van Amstel.

One of those rounded up was Moses Leyden van Amstel, Joop's cousin. After being deported to Mauthausen, 70 of them, probably including Moses, ended up in Hartheim, a killing centre. It was first used for the euthanasia of mentally and physically handicapped people and then experiments were carried out by gassing inmates in the cellars. This was a precursor to the gassing on an industrial scale at Auschwitz and other concentration camps. Relatives back in Holland were told that the deportees had died of pneumonia.

In the second half of 1941, the Joodse Raad (the Jewish Council), established in February 1941, was forced to provide lists of Jews to

Alfred Mossel (Johanna's sister Frederika's husband) sent this picture of Kamp Vladderveen home in May 1942. It was clearly propaganda.

Kamp Vladderveen. The text on reverse of the picture said: 'May 21, 1942, these are our bedrooms, I am not in one of them'.

work in forced labour camps for the German war effort. It seems that one of Joop's uncles Albert Mossel (Joop's mother Johanna's sister Frederika's husband) was at a work camp at Vladderveen for some time before eventually being deported and murdered at Auschwitz. Some of these 'Work Camps' were established in rural areas and were clearly a dry run for the deportation camps that were to open in early 1942.

Albert was allowed to send back photos, which were clearly aimed at being propaganda. They showed neat dormitories and well-organised work. This was an attempt to lure the Jewish population into a false sense of security.

Dutch Jews were well integrated into the Dutch population, having been emancipated as full Dutch citizens in 1795. Dutch society before the Second World War was rather stratified. The main groups, which also held political clout, consisted of two kinds of Protestants – Reformed and Calvinist [*Hervormde* and *Gereformeerde*], Roman Catholics, Socialists and Liberals. Jews did not have any clear representative environment. The Jewish community was itself divided into orthodox, observant, fringe attendees, liberals and socialists.

In January 1942, persecution escalated as the Germans ordered all the Jews in Amsterdam to be confined to one area, to make it easier to deport them. Only certain Jews were not required to do this and Joop's father was temporarily exempt because the Hoogovens did not immediately give in to the demands. In July 1942, the Germans began transporting Jews from Amsterdam to Westerbork, a camp in the north-east of the Netherlands. That was a transit camp and Jews were then transported again to extermination camps in the east.

Both the Dutch civil service and the police actively collaborated and assisted the German authorities in the rounding up of Jews on the streets or in their homes. This was made much easier as the Dutch population registers were very comprehensive and normally indicated religious adherence. Dutch railway workers also administered and operated the trains in which Jews were deported to and from Westerbork and then further to the east.

As Adolf Eichmann fondly recalled at his trial in Jerusalem in 1961: "The trains from Holland – it was a delight." For instance it was most probably a Dutch person who betrayed the Frank family in hiding in Amsterdam, assisted by three Dutch policemen, one of whom was still in the police force in 1980 and who, without a doubt, retired on a full pension.

When I was at school in The Hague the war-time narrative was that the Dutch were better than others who had been occupied by the Germans. After all, even though the Dutch did not prevent the Holocaust, like many of the inhabitants of occupied Europe they stole Jewish property and betrayed Jews to the occupying forces.

The locals did not slaughter their Jewish neighbours, as did happen in Ukraine, Lithuania and Poland. However, the Dutch myth is that they were honest, law-abiding and efficient and that the Germans exploited these characteristics to trick them into deporting Jews.

This was not helped by the fact that the German administration in Holland was in the hands of 'civilian' German administrators, with the experienced Austrian Artur Seyss-Inquart at the head and many other experienced Austrians in charge of various important departments.

In contrast Belgium and France had military administrations, which were often at loggerheads with the Nazi aparachtniks. This resulted in the slaughter of three-quarters of Dutch Jewry.

If you go to the Hollandse Schouwburg, the building where many Dutch Jews were taken after being rounded up, which was once a theatre and is now a memorial to the Dutch victims of the Holocaust, there is a verse:

At home in gathering isolation
Waiting at night in fear
Rounded up by soldiers
Caught in a trap...

Hollandse Schouwburg: from where Dutch Jews were deported.
(Picture: NIOD – Dutch Institute for War, Holocaust and Genocide Studies)

It is actually nonsense. Jews did not sit a home waiting for soldiers. They were collected by Dutch policemen, who were warned that if they did not obey they would lose their Whitsun holiday entitlement.

The senior German police officer in Amsterdam, Hans Albin Rauter, wrote to Himmler in 1942: "Concerning the Jewish Question, the Dutch police behave outstandingly and catch hundreds of Jews day and night."

In the Netherlands there is these days a better understanding of what really happened during the occupation. The myth of a brave people standing up to the German occupiers is now no longer *de rigueur*.

Only a tiny minority of Dutch people lifted a finger to help protect the Jews. My grandmother used to say that those who were at the head of the processions to welcome the German invaders were the same people who were at the front to welcome the liberating Allies! Most of the Dutch population were, often unwillingly, collaborators.

Immediately after the defeat of the Dutch army, some of the discharged soldiers and officers started clandestine resistance. At first this consisted of illegally printing news-sheets that tried to give verified news, rather than the propaganda that the Germans were providing.

Much of this news came via 'Radio Orange' from the BBC in London, which included fiery speeches by the exiled Queen Wilhelmina. She used such strong language that it was said that it was not wise to let your daughters hear her speeches!

'He who acts at the right time, hits the Nazi on the head' [Wie op het juiste ogenblik handelt, slaat den Nazi op de kop]. Hitler she called: 'The arch-enemy of mankind and his gang of criminals' and collaborators were 'utter scoundrels'.

The early attempt at resistance was mainly done by young men in particular, trying to escape to Spain, Sweden, Switzerland and England. This stage of the resistance was rather haphazard and random but soon groups became more organised and were loosely connected as the Order Dienst [Order Service] and they committed sabotage, smuggled weapons, developed espionage techniques and organised illegal telephone connections. In May 1941 the Germans moved against the Order. Its leaders were arrested and ended up in Sachenhausen, where they were executed. As a result of this failure, the underground movement became much more professional. Cell systems were put in place, so that resistance fighters knew as little as possible about each other, so that strings of arrests could not be carried out by the German occupiers.

The accountants firm of Moret & De Jong, where Joop worked, were involved in resistance early on. They were linked with a resistance cell in Leiden. Joop was no longer able to study at the university, work at the accountants, or play for his hockey team, as this was prohibited to Jews. Joop, was involved with the resistance group Stijkel that was connected to Johannes Moret, the head of the accountancy firm, and the group that came from Leiden (I believe a Mrs Pieters was their leader). My father was with Elly and Felix Nauta-Moret (Elly was the daughter of Johannes Moret) and the three of them were fully engaged in resistance work. They gathered espionage material and had weapons and ammunition. All three were involved in the transport of weapons by train to different destinations.

On one occasion in 1941 Joop was taking guns to an area near the German border where he witnessed one of the first RAF bombing raids on the Ruhr, which he described as one of the happiest moments of his life.

Tennis:

A group of students went about giving tennis demonstration matches as cover for transporting guns around the country. I have an envelope dated 1941, addressed to Joop at a hotel in the east of the Netherlands, which I presume was where he was staying in one of his forays to deliver weapons and gather intelligence. Another envelope, also from 1941, addressed to Joop in Zutphen (30km north-east of Arnhem, on the eastern bank of the river Ijssel) where he was staying at a hotel *De Hollandse Tuin*, contains the cryptic message saying: "Will you please inform Mrs S on Friday evening in Bev (Beverwijk?). It has now become very urgent."

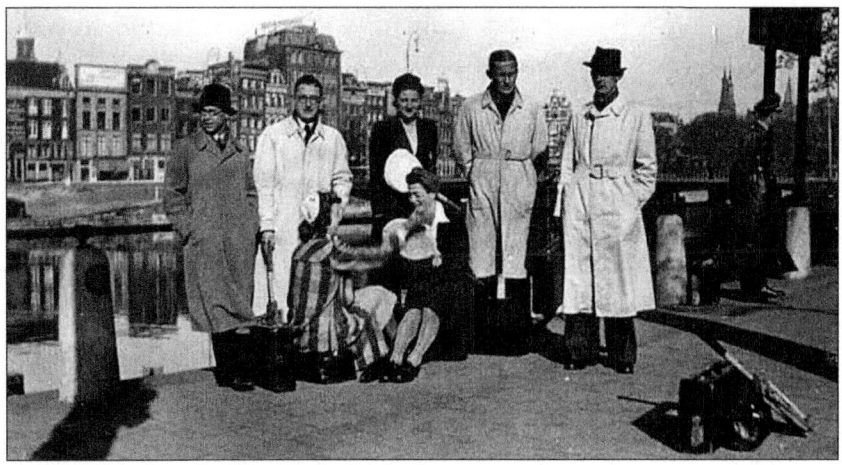

Anyone for tennis? Joop is standing second from left.

The German authorities had forbidden the use of the English terms, love, 15, 30, deuce, etc, but most Dutch clubs defied this by continuing to use those terms. I strongly suspect that Joop and this group were happy to defy the Germans and continue to use English.

At some stage in 1941 he and some friends tried to escape to neutral Spain. They had obtained forged papers saying they were construction workers going to the south of France. They crossed the border to Belgium, walking at night along a railway line, and were hidden by some nuns, until it was safe for them to be taken across the border to France. This obviously accounts for Joop's lifelong soft spot for nuns!

Once in France they travelled by train and were frequently checked by German security. Joop said that the German soldiers were not very bright, because they could easily have seen that they were not construction workers just by looking at their hands, which were very obviously those of students and not builders!

Somehow they managed to get as far as Perpignan where they were arrested and put in a police cell (this was Vichy France) but were shown how to escape by a friendly policeman. They then had to make their way back to the Netherlands, which somehow they managed successfully.

By this time it was pretty obvious that things were hotting up for the resistance group to which Joop belonged. Johannes Moret had been arrested on April 19, 1941 and questioned by the Gestapo, but had been released.

[Later Johannes Moret was 'disappeared' as a '*Nacht und Nebel*' prisoner [Night and Fog], which was a directive issued by Hitler on December 7, 1941 targeting political activists and resistance "helpers" in the territories occupied by Nazi Germany.

They were to be imprisoned, murdered, or made to disappear, while the family and the population remained uncertain as to the fate or whereabouts of the alleged offender against the German occupation power. Victims who disappeared in these clandestine actions were never heard from again. He probably died in Bergen-Belsen.]

Joop, Ellie and Felix were friends and in touch with others who, like them, wanted to escape.

Among them were André and Lou de la Bretionere, brothers born in Tasik on Java in the Dutch East Indies. Both were engineering students. Lou had a political awakening while studying at the Technical Polytechnic in Darmstadt in Germany. He had been picked up by the police a couple of times for mouthing views that were not popular.

In any case, being a young man of Indonesian heritage he was regarded as an 'Untermensch' [sub-human]. Neither he nor his brother could return to the East Indies but were friends with two soldiers of the Dutch East Indian Army, 1st Lieutenant Ferry Meiderts and 2nd Lieutenant Bob van Arem.

Lou, Ferry and Bob were all involved in the early resistance, gathering espionage material and they also had weapons and ammunition. Bob van Arem came to the attention of the Gestapo at some time during 1941 and went into hiding. The three young men undertook a few amateurish escape attempts in the harsh winter of 1941-42. Luckily they were not caught.

In February or March 1942 Ferry Meinderts and Bob van Arem heard on the grapevine of a way to escape from the German occupation – as stowaways on a fishing boat.

Lou trusted unconditionally in his military friends, even though they could not tell him everything, as it had to do with a whole group of people who worked illegally. He waited patiently and got a few visits from a resistance liaison officer, who called himself 'Joosten'. Lou heard from him that they would have to hold up the ship's crew and armed Germans soldiers would probably be on board. They were told to be ready in April. In a briefcase they had espionage reports they had received from Joosten and other paperwork. As a weapon, Lou chose a loaded FN pistol (a Belgian make), in perfect condition, and a hand grenade.

By agreement with Joosten, Lou met his friends, Bob van Arem and Ferry Meyderts, on Monday afternoon, April 6, 1942 at 4pm outside the Hollands Spoor railway station in The Hague. The two, in civilian clothes, had armed themselves. They travelled to Haarlem and went as individuals to a restaurant, looking as normal as possible because there were many German soldiers present.

They waited for a promised contact person from IJmuiden, who would take care of tickets from Haarlem to IJmuiden. Everything beyond Haarlem was *sperrgebiet* (restricted area) and it was only possible to travel with a special permit, for instance as a sailor, or coalbunker labourer. The contact man appeared. He was in possession of a license as a contractor and the three potential escapees were, according to his papers, in his service as coal bunker labourers. The three reached IJmuiden without problem, where their contact took them to a house on the quay.

All this had been made possible because Johannes Moret knew the ship owner, a Mr Taat, who owned the trawler *Katwijk 134* and had permission from the German occupiers to fish at night in the North Sea. With the help of the shore skipper Arie Vooys and a trusted policeman there was a possibility that their escape plan might succeed.

The Spergebiet in Velsen. Homes were demolished to create an open space in case the Allies invaded via Velsen. Louis, Johanna and Joop's home on Zeeweg 80 was demolished. (Picture: From Velsen 1940-1945)

That is where they met the other *Engelandvaarders* [England voyagers] in their group, they were Felix and Elly Nauta-Moret, Joseph Zwalf and Piet Servaas, the latter two both students, and a valiant young Dutchman called Jacob Bakker (known as Bob), an apprentice ship's mate. Bob and Joop had been at school together and were friends from the hockey club.

Elly's father, Johannes Moret, was a partner in the firm of accountants Moret & De Jong, in Rotterdam, was suspected of espionage activities, in which his daughter had participated and was under suspicion by the German police. This made it necessary for Elly and her husband to flee to England.

Johannes knew the owner of the trawler *Katwijk II* and Joop knew a shore skipper, Arie Vooys, who organised fishing boats from the harbour. The ship's owner, J Taat (who had owned the ship since 1933) and Arie Vooys made two promises: the crew of the boat would not be pro-German and the trawler would definitely sail on April 8. What the German armed escort would be like was unpredictable, that is why the escapees would have to be armed.

The escape:

The group agreed in a plan of action. Should the crew after the hold-up not co-operate, Jacob Baker would take over the ship's command as he was an apprentice shipmate. People from IJmuiden, who wished to remain unknown, would provide a way of getting on board. Where the *Katwijk II* exactly was, none of the company knew. Everything depended on blind faith. The password was "How is Marijke?"'. Answer: "Marijke is fine".

At dusk everyone had to leave the house on the quay to be stationed at various shelters along the harbour. A big man in police uniform approached Lou in his hiding place. This was the decisive moment of the whole project, on which it all depended. It could have been a pro Nazi policeman and in these circumstances, at this hour in the harbour at IJmuiden meant arrest and at least internment at Amersfoort. But to his great relief Lou heard the man say: "How's Marijke?"

As far as Lou was concerned all was fine with Marijke! The policeman patted him on the back and went ahead of him across a dark open space to a hangar, the fish hall. The policeman opened a small door. In the middle of the hangar were a couple of shielded lights. Elly, Joop and Piet were already there, lying next to each other on the ground. Not far away they could see light reflecting from the helmets of the German sentries. It was just after 11pm.

The agreement was that if they were caught the men were supposed to be coal bunker workers who were allowed to be in the area and were in the process of sexually assaulting Elly. Lou joined the three of them, waiting for the four other men, who were being brought, one by one, by the policeman. They did not know the policeman, but he was known to Bob Bakker. He revealed in his questioning by the British that it was Johannes Koopman, a policeman in Velsen/Beverwijk/Driehuis. He was, alas, never honoured for his bravery and died in the 1970s.

The next phase of the scheme was to get on board. Joop and Elly went first, and they were spotted by a German soldier, who thankfully ignored them. Joop later said he was the only good German in Holland! The accompanying policeman and Elly then returned to pick up the next man one at a time.

The trawler Katwijk II.

Each man entwined himself with Elly, pretending to be a courting couple, while walking towards a part of the harbour where a number of fishing boats were moored. The *Katwijk II* was moored in the second row with about a metre between it and the first boat, which was immediately next to the quay. Each man was given the message to look for a hatch in the middle of the trawler. Joop guided all of them in, with Elly bringing up the rear. Even though there was a blue light that was screened, it all happened quickly and without attracting attention.

In the hold were creels (wicker baskets used for carrying fish) standing on shelves in compartments. There were loose planks above the keel. This is where the whole group had to crawl in. It was a narrow space, where they could not even stretch their legs. The *Engelandvarders* had seen lots of buckets of ice in the hold, which meant that the trawler was soon to set sail. Once they had closed the planks over their heads all they could do was to await the patrol and beseech all the gods that they would not be discovered. In their confined space there was a sickly and horrible smell of fish. All they could do was to put their circulation into reptile mode, even though peeing was a distinct problem. A shoe had to do as a potty. In the pitch dark and in continuously deteriorating air quality they had to wait the whole night, the next morning and the whole of the following afternoon.

The owner of the *Katwijk II*, Taat had received permission from the Germans to launch his fishing nets between 55km and 65km out. The ship had to leave by 5pm and return by 9am. At 6pm there were at last signs of life. Four or five men stepped on board the trawler and walked about while chatting. The stowaways heard German being spoken. The German patrol only inspected the ship quickly and not too thoroughly. They shone their torches into the hold but did not spot the eight stowaways, who in any case were hiding behind the barrels of ice.

The big question was: would the German patrol stay on board? Then there were more footsteps. Dutch voices now, whistling and laughing. Between 7 and 7.30pm came vibrations and the sound of an engine coming to life. The boat moved. Then there was the sound of lapping waves. Gradually the propeller increased its rpm and after a while the trawler started to heave.

In the hiding place it was nearly intolerable but the group had to wait to make sure they were far enough away from the coast. Even though they had been reduced to suffering wrecks, the stowaway party was ready to act. The morale of the group remained high despite the sea sickness that they had been gripped by. That was all they needed to add to the stench.

The 11-man crew had put out their nets and in the early hours of April 8 the moment arrived, when the trawler anchored. The *Engelandvaarders* had been sitting in their stinking dungeon for two nights and a day. Joop had a lever and as he pushed the plank closure open, lovely fresh sea air blew in. He climbed out followed by Piet Servaas, Ferry Meynderts, Bob van Arem, André and Lou de la Bretonière, Bob Bakker and Felix Nauta. Elly wasn't in any position to stand up and stayed waiting in the hold. Lou immediately fell on his backside while being violently sick but Joop and Piet, with seemingly super human power, remained upright and scrambled in the direction of the bridge.

The mate, Cornelius Guyt, who was on watch, wrote after the war:

[...] Three of us were sitting below decks when someone came stumbling down the steps. We heard immediately that it wasn't any of our crew, so we wondered who it could be. When he got down to us he showed us that he was armed, but we said to him: 'Put that thing away, because we too are Hollanders' [...] What were we to do? On the one hand we would have to leave wives and children behind, but on the other it was our patriotic duty to take these people to the other side. We could have gone back, because they were far too sea sick.

"The trawlermen laughed themselves silly," according to De la Bretoniere 33 years later. "The skipper, Dirk van Duyn, was a great chap. He didn't cause any trouble. But there were a couple of members of the crew who did not want to let their unprepared wives down.

"They said: 'What are we as fishermen to do in England? We hardly speak the language.'

"There was talk of a dinghy on board. One group wanted us to continue our journey in the ship's dinghy, the other wanted the fishermen with objections to return to IJmuiden in the dinghy as so called survivors of a shipwreck.

"Piet Servaas and Joop Zwalf argued against this. With tremendous forcefulness they won the day. They said they could guarantee that they could continue fishing from England and that they would intercede for them with the Queen (Wilhelmina), which they in fact did.

"'We are all in the same boat serving a good cause. Surely you too want the Kraut to get a good beating. And as for your personal situation, Mrs Nauta's father, Mr Moret, is a friend of your ship's owner Mr Taat and they are guarantors that your families will be looked after.'

"So after a few discussions among themselves it was decided to sail on. One of the crew, Gerrit Schaap had to lift two of the *Engelandvaarders* on to the deck, because they were so seasick that they could hardly move."

Piet Servaas wrote about Joop:

"Without him the eight of us would probably never have made it to England. He was the spark plug that kept up our spirits up by talking and joking while we were hiding for more than 24 hours cooped up in the fish hold of the trawler. When it left the harbour it hit the rough open sea and everybody got as sick as a dog. Many were ready to give up.

"But when the time had come a few, with Joop leading the way, scrambled out of the hold on a wildly rolling and tossing deck headed for the bridge, sick as we were. Although the plan was to take control of the ship, as we were well armed, it turned out that the crew could have easily thwarted it and it was Joop who convinced the crew to take us to England. He was our true leader."

Captain van Duyn told them of a number of practical dangers: Naval speedboats and minefields, but he did finally decide to risk it. First they hauled the nets in and then set course for England. Some hours later the Dutch ship came across three English trawlers, who didn't even notice them.

Thanks to Captain van Duyn' s professionalism and seafaring instinct he managed to steer the ship into the channel to Great Yarmouth, without any reaction from the English, who supposed it to be a British trawler. Five kilometres out from Great Yarmouth they raised the Dutch flag and within minutes three shots were fired across the bows. A police boat arrived from the harbour and they heard in Dutch someone shouting: "What do you want here?" The *Katwijk II* followed the police boat into the harbour and tied up to the quay. The crew and the hijackers went to the harbourmaster's office and in due course were arrested and all their possessions were put in sealed bags and the trawler was chained up and guarded.

There was no problem with local police, who kept on at the dozen asking how things were in the Netherlands, while the crew and the hijackers were being regaled with tea and coffee and other delicious treats long since unknown in Holland. Elly was so relieved and happy that she danced on the quayside!

Five of the escapees. Clockwise from top left: Ellie Nauta-Moret, Felix Nauta, Ferry Meinderts, Bob Bakker and Joop Zwalf. The others were: Piet Servaas, André de la Bretionere, Lou de la Bretionere and Bob van Arem.

The Great Yarmouth river frontage of 2024 is not a great deal different to that which greeted the Engelandvaarders in 1942.

Although the warehouse Joop hid in before boarding Katwijk II has been demolished, there are similar warehouses (fish halls) in the background of this 2023 view of IJmuiden harbour.

Once they were transferred to London, *Radio Oranje* sent the following coded message: 'The house with the double shutters: November 27', indicating that all the stowaways had succeeded in reaching England safely.

Mr Moret and his group in the Netherlands then created a whispering campaign to spread the message that the *Katwijk II* had hit a mine and sunk, while telling the wives and families of the crew the opposite. However, because the rumour was that they had all perished at sea, the crews' names were removed from the population registers and a memorial service was held in the church at Katwijk. The 11 crew members, all from Katwijk, continued fishing from Fleetwood in England for the rest of the war, contributing to the Allies war effort!

The *Katwijk II* itself had an interesting history, according to the *fleetwood-trawlers.info* website, which logged it as a wartime visitor to the Lancashire port. Launched in Geestmünde, Germany, in 1905 as the *Gustav Platzmann*, the steam trawler was 116-feet long with a breadth of 22-feet and gross tonnage of 189, destined for a

Stoomtrawler KW134 werd Engelandvaarder

Stoomtrawler KW134 'Katwijk II' verlaat de haven van IJmuiden (Foto: Zee- en Havenmuseum)

A Dutch publication tells the story of the Katwijk II.

(*Picture: The Maurice Voss Collection*)

life fishing the North Sea and Icelandic waters. She became the *Seenelke* in 1908 but was sold the same year and renamed *Senator O'Swald* based in Cuxhaven before being requisitioned by the Imperial Germany Navy for the First World War.

She was abandoned at Zeebrugge during the German evacuation and taken over by the Belgian State and registered as *Yser*. By 1920 she was serving as a pilot boat in Antwerp as *Loodsboot 3*. In 1933 she was sold to Gebroeders Taat in Katwijk and renamed *Antwerp 3*. She was nameless while docked in the Spaarne (a river near Haarlem), before being made ready for fishing in February 1942 and given the name she had when she arrived in England just a few weeks later.

Katwijk II returned to fishing in the Netherlands in August 1945 but was laid up four years later in the herring harbour in

The Katwijk II during her days as Loodsboot 3 in Antwerp during the 1920s.

(Picture: The Maurice Voss Collection)

IJmuiden and broken up in 1951 by demolition company Frans Rijswijk in Hendrik-Ido-Ambacht.

The stowaways were transferred to London where they were interrogated by MI5 at a former girls' boarding school in Wandsworth, south London, which had originally catered for the daughters of soldiers who had died in the Crimean War (1853 -56), the Royal Patriotic School. Apparently this quarantine was not an unpleasant detention. All the foreigners were treated as guests with decent bedrooms, food and drink. There were even newspapers and lectures.

Nevertheless the 'guests' were actually prisoners. They were not permitted any contact with the outside world and were kept there until the authorities were convinced of their political trustworthiness. There were up to 45 interrogators. Every foreigner was questioned in their own language with the most important elements for the interrogators being the back story of the 'guests'.

They wanted background information of where they had

The Royal Patriotic School in Wandsworth, London, where Joop was interrogated. In his notebook he wrote 'on bus route 19'.

(Picture: Laptrinhx.com)

worked, their contacts with the underground, their reasons for escaping. Everyone who had escaped from occupied Europe had to tell in minute detail where they had worked and how they had travelled to work, including the route they took.

Joop said they questioned him in great detail about Velsen/ Beverwijk/Driehius. They asked him to tell them how he would have walked from A to B in Velsen. He said that the interrogators knew every turn and street and even if an empty cigarette packet had been dropped in the streets.

After this he and his fellow escapees were questioned by MI19. MI19 was a section of the British Directorate of Military Intelligence, part of the War Office. During the Second World War it was responsible for obtaining information from enemy prisoners of war and those who had succeeded in escaping from occupied Europe.

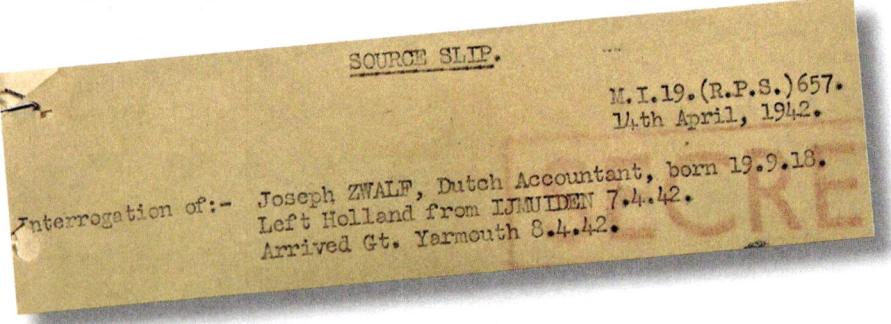

Joop's MI19 interrogation file.
(Picture: The National Archives)

Clearly some of the information that Joop could give MI19 was of interest to the British. His file was distributed to 28 different sections, including: Political Warfare Executive, Military Intelligence, Section 10, [a department of the British Directorate of Military Intelligence, responsible for weapons and technical analysis during the Second World War], Combined Services Detailed Interrogation Centre, Ministry of Economic Warfare, Cmdr Rhodes of US Intelligence, US Navy Intelligence service, and many others.

This is an extract from Joop's interrogation file, taken from The National Archives in Kew:

Information from April 1942:

1. *Informant estimates 3,000 troops in IJmuiden mixed Army and Navy. About two months ago 1,500 men arrived at IJmuiden to bring the figure up to 3,000 total. The new arrivals were mainly elderly troops.*

2. *At the end of March informant spent three days in Leiden and on each of these days he saw a long ammunition train draw into the station. The train was composed of alternating ammunition and coal trucks. The ammunition trucks each carried a red warning flag. In some of the trucks he saw 3ft high aerial bombs packed in industrial cases with their fins projecting.*

3. *On 6.4.42 informant passed through Haarlem and saw a long goods train loaded with damaged heavy armoured cars, medium tanks and other M/T. These vehicles all appeared to have been damaged in action as they had many holes torn in their plating and some were missing wheels. They were camouflaged greenish khaki.*

4. *In March also informant saw a long railway train at Beverwijk passing over the bridge. This train had about 60 trucks and on every two trucks a heavy long barrelled gun was mounted. Informant did not think that they were special railway guns but were simply loaded on to these trucks for transport purposes. He reckoned that there were 30 guns on this train.*

5. *Informant mentioned this train to the station master at Beverwijk who said that there were three others similar to it at Beverwijk. When it was pointed out to informant that those four trains would involve something like 120 heavy guns he stuck to his story. He could not say where the guns were to be mounted, though he had heard of many concrete emplacements being built in the dunes and suggested that the guns would be strung out along the coast.*

6. *Informant could give no first-hand information about the coastal defences but he told two stories received through his father who*

works at the IJmuiden Hoogovens [blast furnaces]. *His father had talked with a workman at this plant, who comes from Wijk aan Zee and he reported that the Germans had laid land mines in the dunes between Wijk aan Zee, Castricum and Egmond aan Zee. Informant could add nothing to this story.*

7. *From the same source he heard that the Germans have built man-high tunnels through the dunes, which debouch on to the beach near Wijk aan Zee and that a new light narrow gauge railway has been laid along the beach between Wijk aan Zee and Castricum. At present this railway is used for carrying building materials and cement to various positions being constructed in the dunes, but it is suggested that it will later be used for taking ammunition to the various gun positions.*

8. *Informant has heard from the Harbour Master of the Fishing Harbour at IJmuiden – a loyal Dutchman- that the Germans have concealed barbed wire defences under water along the coast by IJmuiden. This wire is, according to the Harbour Master, just visible at low water.*

9. *Informant corroborates the story of a general alarm about three weeks ago along the coast of Holland (see MI 19.(R.P.S.) 653) paragraph X (illegible). He confirms that all Germans were called out of cinemas and cafes, but he had heard nothing about civilians having to evacuate the coast. He had heard that the case of the alarm was the dropping of parachutists over Den Helder, The Hague and Rotterdam.*

10. *Informant had been told that there are heavy AA guns in the fields behind Beverwijk railway station. These guns are said to be of French origin and fire in short bursts of 3 rounds at a time.*

11. *Informant's friend the IJmuiden Harbour Master told him that round about March 24 at 1500-1600 hours, three or four E-boats arrived heavily damaged at IJmuiden. One of these, however, exploded and sank just outside the harbour mouth.* [E-boat was the Western Allies' designation for fast attack craft. E-boat could refer to a patrol craft from an armed motorboat to a large torpedo boat.]

12. Informant's secret organisation in Holland had charged him to report as soon as he reached UK that the IJmuiden trawler Y 203 carries a W/T transmitter and 3 or 4 Germans on board and is used as a 'vorposten' [outpost] boat. This information was second hand and informant could only pass it on without corroboration.

13. Informant says that his party were extremely surprised on approaching England to be able to come within one mile of shore without being intercepted at all. They had to attract attention by firing Verey lights and blowing their siren. When they arrived at Great Yarmouth they asked whether their organisation's radio signal about their crossing had been received and they were told that it had come through alright. They were therefore even more surprised not to have been met outside the English coastal minefields. They had fully expected to be piloted safely through the minefields.

14. Informant always listened to the BBC on the 48 metre band. He found this the best for reception at The Hague and IJmuiden. The jamming sounded like bubbling water. He also adopted the common practice in Holland by fitting an extra indoor aerial on the set (see MI 19 (RBS) 653, paragraph 9). Another device to counteract disturbance is known by the Dutch as a "German Filter". This is an arrangement of coils, but informant could not explain it.

15. Informant has never listened through earphones.

16. He believes that the penalty for listening to the BBC is a year's imprisonment. To begin with he always reduced his volume when listening to the BBC as did everyone else, but now people are braver and listen to it at normal volume through loudspeakers.

17. Informant has only heard of one district where Germans have confiscated radio sets, and that is at Maasluis.

18. Informant believes that there is a jamming set at IJmuiden in the farm house of a certain NSB man called Schapp.

19. At the beginning of the Russian war the NSB asked for volunteers to fight in Russia. The response was so slight that now every

NSB man is regarded as a member of the SS and subject to military discipline. To avoid being sent off to the Eastern front many Dutch NSB are trying to get to Belgium to join the NS KK [The National Socialist Motor Corps (German: Nationalsozialistisches Kraftfahrkorps, NSKK) was a paramilitary organisation of the Nazi Party]

20. *Informant had heard that a batch of 200 who did go to Warsaw for training and then on to the front, only 40 returned, and they came back with nothing beyond the clothes they stood up in.*

21. *The informant has heard that the AA guns at Brielle are manned by NSB Dutchmen in the black uniforms of the SS.*

22. *The curfew is now from midnight to 04.00 hours throughout Holland. Station Masters can sign chits to exonerate persons caught out of doors after midnight if the trains have let them down.*

23. *Informant's father works at the Hoogovens in IJmuiden as technical supervisor (see also MI19 (R.P.S. 656). This plant apart from being an important blast furnace produces Azote and ships plates.*

24. *A subsidiary of this company at IJmuiden is one of the biggest cement works in Holland – Cemij (Cement Maatschappij IJmuiden). This cement business is affiliated to another cement works at Maastricht. The share capital of Cemij is however entirely separate from Hoogovens.*

25. *Cement made by Cemij is currently used by the Germans for the fortifications in the dunes.*

26. *The Hoogovens output of pig iron goes to Germany, other products like the plates go to De Muinck Keizer (DEMKA) of Utrecht and Van Leer of IJmuiden.*

27. *Van Leer of IJmuiden also make their own ships plates and girders and iron mesh for Ferro concrete. Van Leer's employ about 1,000 men. Van Leer, being a Jew, left Holland at the earliest moment, and since his departure the firm has been taken over by NV Hoogovens en Staalfabrieken.*

28.   *Hoogovens employ about 1,500 men and part of the share capital is owned by the German concern Gutte Hoffnungs Hutte.*

29.   *The Hoogovens plant is heavily defended by mobile AA guns and searchlights.*

30.   *When the RAF unsuccessfully tried a daylight raid on the Hoogovens a ring from the tail of a British bomb was later picked up by a Dutchman who read thereon the inscription in English- "These are our small bombs; wait till you see the big ones."*

31.   *Cafes in Amsterdam: Germans and NSB men frequent the Cafe Smaalders and the Victoria Hotel near the central railway station.*

32.   *Owing to the shortage of petrol, all German officers must go by train for any journey of more than 75km. This also applies inside Germany.*

33.   *As an indication of Dutch and German nervousness over currency informant quoted the following: the few remaining Old Dutch 10fl gold pieces are now saleable for 78fl paper money.*

34.   *Informant has seen advertisements inserted by Germans in Dutch stamp collectors' magazines offering to buy for high prices English and Canadian stamp collections.*

35.   *The following Amsterdam garages are used exclusively by German military M/T: Trompenburg Garage, Sieberg Garage, RAI Building Garage.*

After having been released by MI5 and MI19, Joop joined the Dutch Army. They had previously rejected him as unfit for military service when he turned 18 in 1936, due to his poor eyesight.

Queen Wilhelmina said of the *Engelandvaarders*: "You are the link between those who stayed behind and me... through you I can gauge the pulse of our people...." Every escapee from Holland was invited to tea with the Queen (of whom Winston Churchill said: "I am scared of no man, except Queen Wilhelmina!"). This consisted of the queen pouring the tea and giving sandwiches

The Bronze Cross
[Het Bronze Kruis].

and cakes to the escapees, talking to each one, asking about their family situation and enquiring about how much information they got from the radio broadcasts sent from England.

These meetings usually took place at her home in Eaton Square and she would frequently take individuals out to the garden so she could talk to them in private, away from her ladies-in-waiting and the adjutants.

On June 11, 1940, Queen Wilhelmina established a bronze cross as an award to officers, NCOs (non-commissioned officers) and men of any of the Netherlands' fighting forces, as well as to those of the Merchant Navy, and to civilians, who distinguished themselves by acts of gallantry or leadership in the presence of the enemy. It was also to be awarded to foreigners who, in so doing, furthered the interests of the Netherlands.

The cross, which corresponds to the British DSC, MC, DSM, and MM, can be given for a single outstanding act, as well as for bravery and enterprise in action over a period. The reverse has the sprays of oak and laurel in the centre, outside the date '1940', and on the four arms the inscription *Trouw-aan-Koningin-en-Vaderland* [Faithful to Queen and Country].

On September 3, 1942, Joop was decorated by Queen Wilhelmina with *Het Bronze Kruis* in recognition of his leadership role and bravery in the escape from Holland.

The citation reads:

"We Wilhelmina, by the Grace of God, Queen of the Netherlands, Princess of Orange Nassau, etc, etc, have approved and undertaken to award the Bronze Cross to Zwalf, Joseph, who in wartime with great care prepared his escape from the land of the Netherlands, occupied by the enemy, which with courage and care organised his crossing to England, which due to the actions of the enemy was accompanied with great danger."

The House with the Double Shutters

I n January 1941 Queen Wilhelmina conferred the title *Koninklijke Nederlands Brigade Prinses Irene* [The Royal Netherlands Princess Irene Brigade] on the unit and in August the same year presented it the brigade standard.

Those who could fly went off to form the Dutch arm of the Royal Air Force and others were selected for special training with the SAS (Special Air Service), initially formed as a commando force – and SOE (Special Operations Executive) – working in espionage for service overseas, organising resistance behind enemy lines.

A camp was built for the Dutch brigade at Wrottesley Hall, a country estate west of Wolverhampton, (just imagine Dutch soldiers trying to pronounce 'Wrottesley!), under the command of Lt Col AC de Ruyter van Steveninck. During the following two years the brigade trained as a unit and performed coastal defence duties on the Essex coast in Harwich, Frinton-on-Sea and Dovercourt. It was here that Joop had his basic military training and was selected to be parachuted back into the Netherlands to support the underground.

Special Operations Executive:

The SOE was a British Second World War organisation. It was officially formed on July 22, 1940 under the Minister of Economic Warfare, by the Eton-educated socialist Hugh Dalton, from the amalgamation of three existing secret organisations. Its purpose was to conduct espionage, sabotage and reconnaissance in occupied Europe and to aid local resistance movements.

Few people were aware of SOE's existence. Those who were part of it or liaised with it were sometimes referred to as the 'Baker Street Irregulars', after the location of its London headquarters. It was also known as 'Churchill's Secret Army' or the 'Ministry of Ungentlemanly Warfare'. The branch that dealt with the Netherlands was 'N Section' but it was singularly lacking in understanding of the Netherlands, the most densely populated country in Europe.

It was difficult to move round the country unobserved, not least because of the excellent railway and road system that meant the Germans and police agents could move round the country with ease and reach virtually anywhere in a few hours. In addition it was virtually impossible to land agents on the Dutch coast, which had no hidden coves or harbours.

The beaches were heavily mined and defended with concrete blocks and German sentries. N Section seemed pretty clueless about what was happening in The Netherlands and did not appreciate the difficulties facing agents and members of the Dutch resistance. In September 1941 two operatives made it to the Netherlands, who were supposed to recruit Dutch citizens to the resistance. They were meant to be picked up by boat several weeks later but no rendezvous ever took place and, because they had no radio to contact London, they soon disappeared.

In November SOE tried again by parachuting two Dutch men, who had been trained as wireless operators, into the Netherlands with the task of setting up new resistance networks and training members of the underground in sabotage techniques. However, London heard nothing from them until January 1942. They sent regular reports of the work they were doing but eventually Leo Marks, in N Section, found a major mistake in their work.

One of them began omitting their security check, which they had to do to show that they had not been captured and were not working under the control of the Germans. Marks was, however, over-ridden and told that there was nothing to worry about. Actually the agents were in a Gestapo prison in The Hague, the so-called 'Oranje Hotel'. The whole operation had been handled with appalling casualness. The forged documents they carried were on the wrong kind of paper and although their clothes had Dutch labels sown into them, their style clearly shouted 'England'. The coins they used in a cafe had been taken out of circulation some time earlier.

Once they had been captured by the *Abwehr* [German counter intelligence] they tried to warn London by omitting their security code and when there was no reaction from London they even tried inserting 'CAU' and 'GHT' into their messages to warn London, who gave no indication that they understood.

When a new operative was parachuted to the Netherlands the Germans were there to welcome him. From March 1942 onwards a steady stream of operatives and weapons were dropped into the waiting arms of the *Abwehr* and the Gestapo.

This was *das Engelandspiel* [the England Game] organised by Major Hermann Gilkes of the *Abwehr* that cost the lives and capture of some 50 operatives, including Joop's school friend and fellow escapee Bob Bakker. Most of this abject disaster was caused by SOE's N Section and convinced the Germans that the whole operation was run by a bunch of amateurs. In turn they outwitted the captured agents, implying that there was a double agent in SOE who was betraying them to the Germans.

Despite Leo Marks bringing attention to the head of N Section that the security codes were never entered in the messages from the Netherlands. Pilots ferrying the agents to be dropped in Holland always had an easy flight with landing sites well laid out and lit but on the way back anti-aircraft guns were blazing – but never on the way there. As one pilot is alleged to have said it was: "Too bloody perfect."

On June 26, 1942, an agent and a wireless operator and several tons of weapons and explosives were parachuted into Holland and met by a large German welcoming party. London finally began to take notice towards the end of 1942. It was perhaps this occasion that Bob Bakker was parachuted back.

In the meantime, Joop was being trained as an agent to also be parachuted back 'home' to support the resistance. His training was originally in Wrottesley followed by parachute training in Scotland. The parachute practice jumps were over the islands of Rum, Muck and Eigg off the west coast of Scotland. On one of these drops Joop broke a leg on landing and had to crawl and hop for 12 hours to the rendezvous point.

His training must have ended towards the summer of 1942

and he was ready to be dropped back into the Netherlands. The drop before his one had been picked up by the Germans and the Dutch government in exile was suspicious and Joop's drop was cancelled.

All 54 agents who had been sent to the Netherlands by SOE had been captured and had been promised eventually to be set free. However, as the Allies closed in on the Netherlands, they were all sent to the Mauthausen concentration camp in Austria and 50 of them were machine gunned to death. Only four survived.

After his commando training in Scotland and there being no possibility of returning to the Netherlands to support and intensify the resistance, Joop volunteered to be sent to the Dutch East Indies, which had been overrun by Japanese forces shortly after the fall of Singapore.

In the meantime, Joop and at least one other were billeted in the Bangor Hotel, at 36 Bedford Place, London, WC1.

Joop and his companions, Jules Bastiaans, Pieter du Bus de Valenpre and Huibert Staverman, boarded a Blue Star Line ship being used as a troop ship, the SS Australia Star, from Liverpool to Australia, via the Panama Canal.

Joop joked that when the ship passed the Virgin Islands the ship nearly capsized due to all the soldiers hanging over the side of the ship in hope that they could spot one!

The liner had been designed to ship frozen meat from Australia and New Zealand to the United Kingdom. She had a distinguished role during the war in the relief of the siege of Malta in August 1942 but was sunk by a torpedo in 1943 near Bermuda with the loss of 115 lives.

Soon after the evacuation from the Dutch East Indies, a Dutch intelligence service was set up in Australia, based in Melbourne on

The SS Australia Star.

Panama City, September 11, 1942. Back, from left: Jim Perry, Pieter du Bus de Valenpre, 'Spark'. Front: Jules Bastiaans and Joop Zwalf.

the instructions of the Dutch Government in Exile. Netherlands East Indies Forces Intelligence Service (NEFIS) was a Dutch Second World War intelligence and special operations unit, operating mainly in the Japanese-occupied Netherlands East Indies including Dutch New Guinea (now part of Indonesia).

NEFIS I gathered reports, maps, publications and photos on the Dutch East Indies. On the basis of this information, monthly summaries were issued on the situation in the archipelago. NEFIS II was responsible for censoring the mail of Royal Netherlands Navy and Royal Netherlands East Indies Army (KNIL – [*Koninklijk Nederlandsch-Indisch Leger*] Royal Dutch-East Indies Army) personnel. It also checked whether the spouses of Dutch troops in Australia presented a security risk.

It was not involved in carrying out secret intelligence operations. That was the task of the Inter-Allied Services Department (ISD), that had been set up in April 1942 on the instructions of US General Douglas MacArthur and was responsible for sending out agents to commit sabotage and gather intelligence in occupied areas. Two Dutch officers were assigned to the Dutch East Indies section, which, like NEFIS, was based in Melbourne.

A few months later, on July 6, 1942, the Inter-Allied Services Department was merged with other intelligence services operating from Australia. The Dutch section of the former ISD was incorporated into this division. The Dutch section carried out various operations in enemy territory. NEFIS was not given the task of sending agents on assignments until after the AIB had been reorganised in April 1943.

A new division, NEFIS III, was created for this purpose in May 1943. It sent secret agents into occupied territory by submarine or aeroplane to gather intelligence on the local political and military situation. If possible, these agents had to make contact with the local population to gather information and set up undercover organisations. It is to this group that Joop was assigned on his arrival in Australia.

NEFIS III had little success with the deployment of secret

agents. Despite the training course, the agents lacked experience and expertise. It was also difficult to win support from the local population in the Dutch East Indies, as they feared Japanese reprisals. NEFIS III, and its predecessor, the Dutch section of the ISD, sent 36 teams into enemy territory. More than 250 agents were involved in these operations, and 39 lost their lives.

Joop usually had six weeks on operations in New Guinea and six weeks off in Melbourne. They would be flown in Dakotas from Essendon Airport in Melbourne to Darwin and then by submarine to New Guinea. Joop occasionally told of disrupting Japanese communications by disabling telegraph posts but, as usual about most of his war experiences, he was more or less silent.

Landing in New Guinea from a submarine, May 1944.

I t is thought that Louis knew of Joop's successful escape and Johanna possibly knew, but this is by no means certain.

Louis was involved in an effort to arrange for Jewish children to be 'adopted' by gentile families. This was organised through the Trade Union at the Hoogovens. Not much is known about this attempt, or how successful it was.

In the Netherlands the persecution developed slowly, with new anti-Jewish laws being promulgated every few weeks. In July 1942, Jews aged 16 to 35 were ordered to report mostly to their local train stations to be sent to destinations in Germany for forced labour. There, many of the young Jews were murdered immediately upon arrival.

Joop's cousin Jaap de Zoete, with a friend. They did not know they were on their way to be murdered.

As 1942 progressed, many Jews sought to evade the deportation orders by hiding. These Jews now also included the old, the ill, and the mentally handicapped, who the Germans had begun to deport as well.

Parents' decisions about hiding their children was not an easy one for several reasons. First, as of July 1942, there was no organised underground network for hiding children. Second, Jews' identity cards carried a large black 'J' that could not easily be removed (children aged six and younger did not need an identity card). Third, a place was needed where the children could hide. Finally, hiding children required at least a little money, sometimes a lot. Not every hiding family could handle the costs and some demanded payment as compensation.

By the end of 1942 an underground network was more or less functioning, but by that time much of Dutch Jewry had already been murdered. The young people, many of them being students from Amsterdam and other universities, who belonged to the underground organisations, tried to persuade remaining parents to send their children into hiding. These were difficult conversations because the idea of relinquishing their children obviously distressed the parents. They did not know where they would be sent, whether they would be safe, whether the strangers would care for them well, or how much the children would suffer from the sudden total separation from their parents. Often the underground members were sent away empty-handed.

The people who took the heavy risks of hiding Jews often did not realise the sorts of punishments the Germans could mete out to them upon discovery. Many were killed, sent to concentration camps, or had their homes and belongings burned. Hiding Jews also entailed grave consequences for their familial and social life. Their children were generally forbidden to speak about the "guest" and could not bring friends home from school; often the families themselves could not receive visitors. Moreover, food and clothes became scarce and families had limited resources and needed ration cards for food.

Louis and Johanna in early 1940.

Louis' arrest:

By the summer of 1942 Louis was well aware of the dangers that were all around and on a trip to Amsterdam on September 18, visiting Johanna's sister, they arrived at Centraal Station and made their way along Prins Hendrikkade – a major street in the centre of the city. It was always their plan that they would walk on opposite sides of the road, so that if one of them was stopped the other could carry on. Louis was stopped by two policemen.

The police report read:

> *"12 noon, the police constables Knoop (3328) and Tilkera (5789) on duty at 6/1 on the Prins Hendrikkade brought a Jew, named Levie Zwalf, born Amsterdam March 17 1889, by profession electrician, living in Velsen at Zeeweg 80 red.*

> *"The named Jew was walking without a jewstar (star of David, pictured above right) and had arrived in Amsterdam without a travel permit. He is kept in custody for arraignment before the SD (Sicherheitsdienst– [the SS intelligence agency]). Zwalf had also messed with his identity card by removing the J."*

Louis would have been locked up in one of the cells in the cellar of the SD building, which had previously been a girls' high school and, after having been interrogated, transferred to the detention centre known as the *Weteringschans,* the former House of Detention.

The notorious House of Detention (Weteringschans) on the Kleine-Gartmanplantsoen. Below a modern view of the front of the same building.

Situated on *Kleine-Gartmanplantsoen*, it was a notorious prison during the Second World War. Anne Frank and her family were imprisoned there for two days, before they were deported to Westerbork.

From the summer of 1942 as the deportation were beginning, the day reports of the Amsterdam police have numerous mentions of 'Jews and Jewesses', who just like Louis were not wearing a Star of David or did not have permission for whatever and were being picked up and transferred via the Bureau of Jewish Affairs to the SD.

Already on July 25, Jetta Zwalf-Barnstein and her husband, Louis' brother Hartog (Hendrik), had reported to the police that their daughter Hanna, who had been working as a housekeeper, had disappeared. The policeman on duty noted 'she was very nervous and fears that her daughter has had an accident'. She had gone into hiding!

Kamp Amerfoort:

Louis was probably transferred in late September or early October to the newly opened concentration camp at Amersfoort before the new camp was constructed at Westerbork

In May 1941 the *Sicherheitsdienst* (SD, the intelligence organisation of the SS) occupied the camp, which in pre-war days had been an army training camp. The SD requisitioned the camp in order to turn it into a *schutzhaftlager* (a camp to keep prisoners in captivity as protection). Because of the strongly growing number of prisoners as a result of the Nazi rule, the regular prisons were filled to the brim and other places for prisoners had to be found. One of the new locations to keep prisoners in custody was *Barakkenkamp Appelweg*, commonly known as *Kamp Amersfoort*. The name was then changed into *Polizeiliches Durchgangslager Amersfoort* (PDA). This name was changed into *Erweitertes Polizeigefängnis Amersfoort* [Expanded Police Prison] in spring 1943.

The history of the camp can be separated into two periods. The

Kamp Amersfoort.
(Picture: NIOD – Dutch Institute for War, Holocaust and Genocide Studies)

first began on August 18, 1941, and ended in March 1943. In March 1943 all but eight of the surviving first prisoners in Amersfoort were transferred to Kamp Vught. The prisoner transfer to Vught allowed for the completion of an expansion of Kamp Amersfoort.

As Louis had been handed over to the SD by the Amsterdam police he was transferred to Kamp Amersfoort, probably in September 1942. Many of the prisoners there were sent to Germany as compulsory labour. The fluctuating prisoner population consisted of people from all over the Netherlands: Jews, Jehovah's Witnesses, prisoners of war from the Soviet Union, members of the resistance, clergy, black marketers, hostages, clandestine butchers and smugglers. Between 1941 and 1943, about 30,000 people were imprisoned in the camp, of whom 20,000 were deported to Germany.

A Roman Catholic priest, Father van Genuchten, describes the 'welcoming ceremony' to the camp , which he and 130 other prisoners underwent in September 1941"

"Los, los, rauf, lauf, lauf' [Go, go, up, run, run], the doors
were opened and we were driven out of the trucks with canes
beating us. When we arrived at the assembly square, the
prisoners had to take their clothes off and run between two
rows of SS soldiers. They were armed with sticks and hit us
wherever they can."

An illegal worker relates how the *kapos* [a functionary who was a trusted prisoner in a Nazi camp who was assigned by the SS guards to supervise prisoners] made them run, fall, get up, roll sideway on the ground, get up, lie down, all at double quick pace for hours on end. Those who couldn't keep up were pitilessly beaten with clubs.

It was on July 15, 1942, that the Germans began deporting Dutch Jews from Amersfoort, Vught and Westerbork to concentration camps and death camps such as Auschwitz, Sobibor and Theresienstadt.

Most of the Jewish prisoners at Amerfoort were transferred to Westerbork, which was an in-between camp on the way to the extermination camps. Louis was transferred to Westerbork on December 8, 1942 with 72 other Jewish prisoners.

Westerbork:

Kamp Westerbork was built in 1939 as a camp for German and Austrian legal and illegal Jewish refugees who had fled their countries to the Netherlands. The first 22 Jewish refugees arrived there in October 1939. On October 14 the Dutch newspaper *De Telegraaf* in an article with photographs reported 'A town in concept in the heath lands of the province Drente'.

The article described the barracks as having curtains embroidered with flowers and it appeared that in the long term there were substantial plans afoot, although it was a long way to the east (just a few miles from the German border) and it was isolated 'so far away that the morning post delivery only gets there at 4pm'. It was designed for 3,000 inhabitants and the article went on to describe the camp as 'nice, fresh and healthy'. By the time that the Germans invaded in May 1940 there were 750 Jewish refugees there.

In fact, according to a member of the Dutch Parliament in early 1940, Kamp Westerbork was about 60 acres of 'barren desolate plain in the most depressing area in our country. It is flat and therefore open to the wind, the peat land is boggy and damp and it is isolated and one of the only places in our country of which one could say it was God forsaken'.

After the invasion, the camp continued to be run by the Ministry of Justice until July 1942 when the Germans took over control and changed it from the Central Refugee Camp to a Police Detention Centre. The refugees realised that this was a doom shattering change of name. Even for Jews in Amsterdam the alarm bells started ringing, especially as Westerbork was now surrounded by barbed wire. Panic ensued in the camp and two weeks later it turned out not to be a false alarm as the first group had to walk the mile or so to the station at Hooghalen where the cattle truck were ready to transport them to 'the East' arriving in Auschwitz on July 18, 1942. Awaiting them there was Heinrich Himmler.

Rudolf Hoess, camp commandant at Auschwitz recalled:

> "After the visit to Birkenau he himself sampled the process of the annihilation of one recently arrived Jewish transport, which he watched in complete silence
>
> "Later he and his party and the camp officials sat down to a meal. Himmler was at his best, in radiant mood; he led the conversation and was extremely amiable... he spoke about all sorts of subjects... about bringing up children and new homes and paintings and books...
>
> "As for those on the transport: may they rest in peace."

However, when Louis arrived in Westerbork he must have been delighted to leave the wretched regime at Amerfoort. On arrival he was admitted to the hospital there, clearly quite badly

Kamp Westerbork.
(Picture: NIOD – Dutch Institute for War, Holocaust and Genocide Studies)

injured but able to recuperate from the hard physical labour and lack of food. There is a terrible irony that the Germans cared for the inmates so well in the hospital in Westerbork only to deport them to be murdered.

While Louis was in Westerbork he was visited by an old school friend of Joop's, Henk Stol. After the war he wrote to Joop:

> *"Now I will redeem a promise. My visit to Westerbork. At your request, the truth; the naked truth. Before I visited there I made enquiries and found out some addresses of people who would be prepared to risk life and limb to shelter your father and arranged that the van der Werf family in Veenhuizen were prepared to shelter your father. Then I went to reconnoitre the area around the camp to look for possible ways to escape. This wasn't easy as you can imagine, but it was not without possibility.*
>
> *"If I were to wait at a certain point the following night or the night following that with two bicycles there would have been reasonable chance that we could have succeeded and that we could have reached the safe house. When visitors, who were*

allowed to visit the prisoners in the barracks, were admitted, the prisoners were let in one by one by other Jews who were in charge of them.

"When the name 'Zwalf' was called, I had already secured a space, which was pretty separate, at the far left back of the room, so that I could talk quietly with your father. It was lovely to see him again. Your father had lost weight of course, and his face was much more drawn than before. But then he was never ever plump in the face.

"His first reaction was: 'Bloody hell, Stol, what are you doing here? He always called me by my surname. But after our first words he called me by my first name and me him, something neither of us had done before and I don't know why we did.

"When I asked him how he was, he told me that he had no particular complaints about Westerbork but he did say terrible things about the previous camp at Amersfoort when he had been first detained; he had been beaten up so often that he thought he might die. He showed me his head and neck, where there were scars that have only recently healed. His legs and feet too were covered in scars, which had been made by blows with sticks and whips. But when I saw him he had no open wounds.

"He told me how they had to crawl through mud on hands and feet. And if they were not fast enough the whips and stick were brought out on blows and kicks were aimed at their bodies. But your father was not down, but then that was not, I believe, a characteristic that he had!

"As time was limited, in fact we have no idea how long we would be able to talk; we did not discuss his experiences further, and in any case that was quite unnecessary if you could have seen him. But I can say that he was not a broken man, which was obvious when I whispered to him my plans to help him escape. He did hesitate, but his confidence in his own body made him decide that, as he said: 'I have survived Amersfoort and so I will survive Poland too'.

"You must remember that at that time not much was known about Poland. There were rumours of zinc and mercury mines and gas chambers but no one knew anything for certain and everyone thought, your father included, that these rumours were greatly exaggerated. No one had ever returned from Poland to tell.

"Your father asked after your mother, who by then was hiding in Hoorn, and asked after you and Ank and my parents. I told him of a Red Cross letter from you that had been received.

"When he was called away we kissed, which seems strange but then you and I and embraced each other on the dark jetty wall in IJmuiden the day you escaped to England.

"I hope that your father enjoyed my visit and that it cheered him up a bit. I was, I admit, disappointed that he did not want to risk escaping as I think it might have been worth a try. But the decision was his.

"From a friend in the police I heard how the worst moment was when a transport was to leave; those dirty rotten Krauts stuffed an unbelievable number of people in each wagon.

Dear Joop, these are my memories of my visit to your father in Westerbork, I shall always have a wonderful memory of him, and the picture of him, which I carry in my mind, I shall have with me for the rest of my life. He was a fine man."

Henk Stol:

Henk visited Louis in Westerbork, and he mentions that there might be a place he could be hidden in Veenhuizen – about 30km from Westerbork. Henk Stol wrote the letter in September 1947 when talk of deportations and the persecutions of Jews was not spoken about and indeed the war was hardly ever mentioned.

He actually heads his letter to Joop: 'Not for further publication'. Henk also said that Johanna was hiding in Hoorn, which as far as is known was never the case. However, it is more likely that Henk did not know exactly where she was being hidden as he was also a member of the underground resistance and if caught it would have been safer if he did not know exactly where she, or anyone else for that matter, was being hidden.

Henk was associated with the student-led underground group around Sjoerd Nauta.

L ouis' possibly optimistic view of his 'resettlement in the East' was not unusual. Rumours did circulate, however, in fact Anne Frank in her diary wrote:

October 9, 1942

Dearest Kitty,

Today I have nothing but dismal and depressing news to report. Our many Jewish Friends and acquaintances are being taken away in droves. The Gestapo is treating them very roughly and transporting them in cattle cars to Westerbork, the big camp in Drenthe to which they're sending all the Jews.

Miep told us about someone who'd managed to escape from there. It must be terrible in Westerbork. The people get almost nothing to eat, much less to drink, as water is only available one hour a day, and there's only one toilet.

Escape is almost impossible; many people look Jewish, and they're branded by their shorn heads. If it's that bad in Holland, what must it be like in those faraway and uncivilised places where the Germans are sending them?

We assumed that most of them are being murdered. The English radio says that they are being gassed. Perhaps that's the quickest way to die.

Perhaps Louis had not heard these rumours, but after all they were just rumours and he was a skilled professional electrician who had held a responsible job at the Hoogovens. Perhaps there was a job in 'the East'.

The Nazi regime throughout Europe talked only of Jewish 'resettlement in the East' and they deceived their victims constantly on an industrial scale. They lied to their victims every step of their journey to destruction.

Those boarding the trains and cattle trucks believed that they were being taken to a new life in the East. The Jews on the trains packed up their belongings thinking that they were building a new home where they would need pots and pans, clothes to wear and toys for their children.

They believed this because that it what the Germans had told them and some had even received postcards, which they did not realise had been written at gunpoint.

The deception was carried on even after the wagons were opened up as they arrived in Auschwitz. The SS would pretend that the horrendous journey that they had endured was some kind of aberration.

Those transported from Westerbork (or Paris, or Mechelen in Belgium, or Slovakia, etc) were raised to expect the best from civilised Germans. At last they had arrived and could expect accommodation, food and respite. The pretence continued, the SS men with impeccable manners would help the infirm on to trucks that would take them to be murdered.

For those who were going to their death on foot there was reassurance, they were asked about their jobs and qualifications back home, which must have meant that their skills were to be used.

If they asked about where they were going they were told, 'for disinfection'. After all, the entire journey had been horrid and squalid, so that made sense. Even the execution site was disguised. It looked like a farmhouse next to two wooden huts for undressing, and by the crematoria there were flower beds. These were the deportees' final minutes, but the Nazis encouraged them to believe that they still had a future.

Their victims followed the order to strip off their clothes and the SS would tell them that they were about to bathe and that afterwards there would be coffee and food to eat. They even reminded their victims to tie their shoes together in pairs so that they would not be lost. The SS knew perfectly well that the shoes of murdered children would be of use to families back home in Germany. When they were pushed inside the gas chambers the deception did not end even there. Signs said: 'To the baths' and there were fake shower heads in the ceiling.

It was essential that the Jews coming off the trains did not know the fate that awaited them. If they did they might cry out, create a stampede, might not be willing to form columns in rows of five and might rush at their captors.

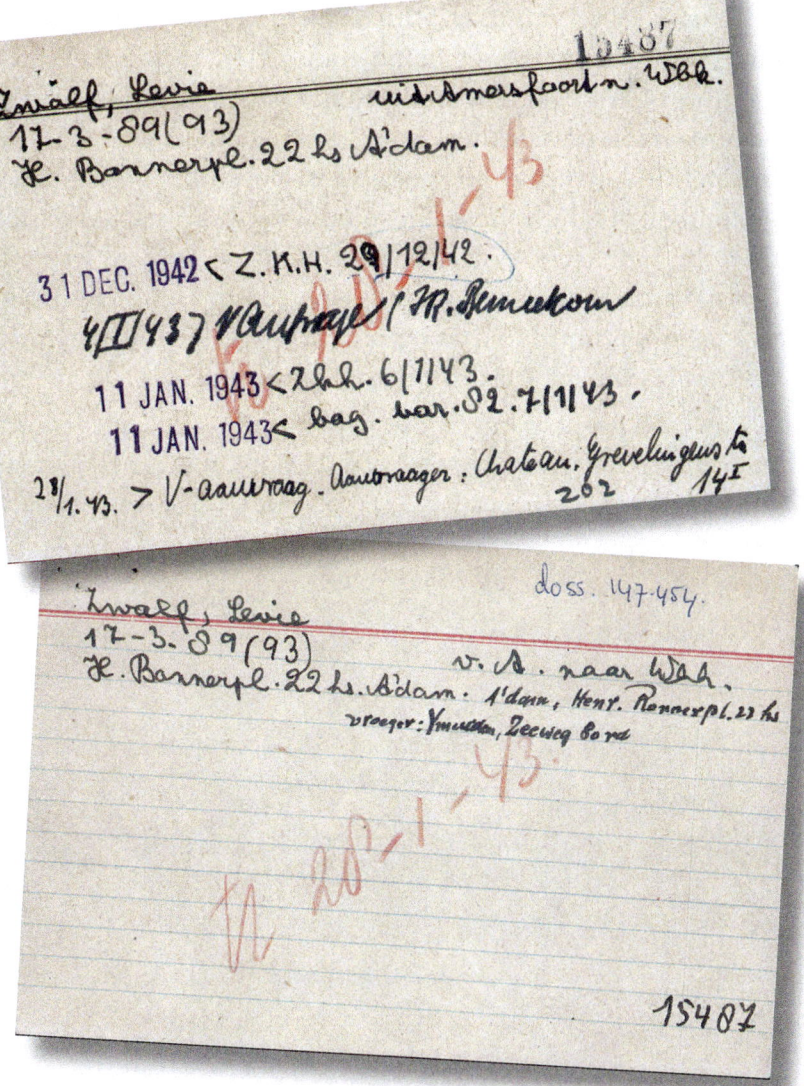

The Jewish Council's registration card for Louis.

(Picture: Arolsen Archives)

Of course they would eventually be overwhelmed by the SS who after all carried sub machine guns but they might have delayed the murders even though they were outnumbered.

They might slow it down but they could not stop it. The deception had to be kept up from beginning to end, if the extermination process was to be a success.

Louis' registration card, which is kept at the Arolsen Archives and is in the process of being transferred to the Netherlands Institute of War Documentation and Holocaust Studies, says that he appears in the 'sickness book' at Amersfoort and that he was transferred to Westerbork, possibly in December 1942 and that on December 29 he was in the hospital wing at Westerbork and still there on January 6, 1943. The card indicates that he was put on transport on January 23, was transported by train to Auschwitz, where he was murdered on January 26, 1943. The card says that he was not present at Westerbork on February 1.

The card has a red inscription: 'to (?) 28-1-43'. The Netherland Institute of War Documentation does not know exactly what this

Transport from Westerbork to Auschwitz.

means, but probably that Westerbork was notified on January 28 that he had been 'eliminated'.

The transports East from Westerbork in January 1943 were:

January 11 – 750 people; January 18 – 748; January 21 – 921

January 23 – 515; January 29 – 869

These transports seem not to have been the only ones. It is not certain on which transport Louis was put. According to the Institute of War Documentation it was January 26, camp Westerbork claims it was January 28 and according to the Red Cross it was January 29.

Leon Greenman, who was either on the same transport as Louis or on the one before, wrote in his book: 'An Englishman in Auschwitz:

> "It was January 1943 and snow was on the ground as we stood queuing for the train. Prisoners at Westerbork had completed the rail line to the camp ... so at least we didn't have to endure the long march that had brought us here.

> "We slowly made our way towards the train. As we approached I saw two men standing on the platform – SS Commander Konrad Gemmecker, the German commander at Westerbork and Kurt Schlesinger, wearing his trademark jackboots. [Schlesinger was a German Jew who ran the administration at Westerbork] ... As we boarded the train, orders were shouted for those not leaving on the transport to go into their barracks and not come outside again...

> "There were eight of us in our compartment, sitting opposite one another in two rows. It was nearly 11 o'clock in the morning when the train steamed out of the camp. Now all we could do was wait and see what would happen. We had been told that we were being sent to Poland to work for the Germans... We thought we would get through it and start our lives anew after the war. We could only hope that the war would end soon. We talked during the 36-hour trip to Poland. The train moved slowly and stopped at various places along the way. We could

not see out as the windows were covered up. We were not permitted to leave our compartment and we had nothing to eat or drink.

"We were tired, hungry, miserable and utterly hopeless, moving to a destination unknown. All that we had worked for... had been taken from us because we had been born Jewish.

"Eventually the train stopped. We had arrived at a place we had never heard of before. It was Birkenau. Then a loud voice shouted in German: 'Raus, raus! Alles lassen liggen!' [Get out, get out! Leave everything!]. We were shocked, bewildered and tired. We all started to move out of the train. It was cold, dark, early morning. There we stood on the snow-covered platform; all our luggage left on the train.

"The women were separated from the men. Here I was, standing among the men, total strangers. Suddenly I saw a woman run towards us – to her husband – shouting hysterically. And then, before my eyes, a big SS officer lifted his club and beat her round the head several times. Down she went, and he kicked her in the body. Stepping over her, the SS officer came towards us and separated 50 men from the rest of the group. I was chosen. I wondered what was going to happen next."

Louis was not one of those 50.

During the Second World War 'Going into hiding' [*onderduiken* 'to dive under'] took on a new meaning. It came to mean finding a secret place to live so that one could remain out of the Germans' hands.

During the course of the war the number of those in hiding increased dramatically. The first people to go into hiding were Dutch Jews who were escaping their deportation. People who were in the resistance and who were being sought went into hiding too. In addition there were young men who refused to work for the Germans, either in the Netherlands or Germany.

In February 1941, the German Reichskommissar in Holland, Seyss-Inquart, proclaimed an ordinance concerning the "duty for the performance of services". This order provided for the forced employment of Dutch citizens in Nazi Germany and its occupied territories. The recruitment took place initially through regional Dutch government employment offices that possessed the means for enforcement, specifically in the case of unemployed persons.

More than 500,000 Dutch citizens were forced to work in Germany during World War Two. More than 30,000 of them perished through hunger, sickness, mistreatment and acts of war. In 1944 more were added to the number, when railway workers, who were on strike, went into hiding. It was never easy to find enough addresses to go into hiding. In addition one had to be able to hide if raids or house searches were threatened. At the slightest rumour the person hiding had to disappear under the floorboards, behind a cupboard, in the cellar or wherever. In rural places like Heemskerk there were possibilities.

The resistance in Velsen/IJmuiden:

Already by 1941 there existed a framework of illegal underground work in Velsen, organised by different resistance groups that had originated in Sandvoort, which was beyond the *Sperrgebiet* [the fortress, restricted area]. The Netherlands was strongly compartmentalised before the war and developed separate resistance groups of Protestant, Roman Catholic, Socialist and

Communist sympathies, who as the war progressed learned to work together more and more.

In 1941 a former army officer set up the 'V Leger' (the freedom or resistance army), who were mainly concerned with military espionage, sabotage and assassinations. The 'citizens department' helped Jews to hide.

Dirk van Rijswijk and Frederik Hendrik van Dijk, alias De Wit, were two early members of this group. The group's headquarters was a house owned by a man who owned a food business and members were active in stealing food coupons and food for those in hiding as well as trying to free prisoners and commit sabotage.

A Roman Catholic Capuchin monk, Fr Pontianus and some of his fellow monks created a resistance group with some young men in IJmuiden. Together they hid people as well as weapons, resistance material and those who temporarily needed a roof over their heads. They hid them in the attic of the Franciscan School and under the floor of the adjacent nursery. A 15-year-old Jan van Breemen, who worked at the food business, knew a number of Jewish families and tried to persuade them to go into hiding, sometimes in vain and sometimes with success. He helped a girl, Anneke Menist, to hide with the sisters of the St Anthony Hospital. It helped that Jan's father was the police watch commander in Velsen and could let Fr Pontianus know about the activities of the fanatical SS and NSB members of the police.

Johanna goes into hiding:

Johanna had seen Louis' arrest taking place from the other side of the road and must have made her way back to Velsen and made contact with Frederik Hendrik van Dijk, whom she probably knew from Joop and Levie's contact with the underground.

He was an early linchpin in the local group of the underground helping both Jews and others to hide from the Germans. To start with she was hidden in Beverwijk. By May 1943 it was no longer safe and in the middle of the night two women from the resistance took her by a circuitous route to Heemskerk to the Borst Family.

The daughter of the family, Jane, was five years old and recounts how her mother told her that 'Tante Jo' had come to help her with the housekeeping. In fact 'Tante Jo' made clothes for the children and made a doll for Jane out of rags.

The children loved her: Jane called her a 'golden angel'. Mrs Borst, however, was always terrified of being caught sheltering a Jewish lady.

Jane says that Tante Jo was in great uncertainty about the fate of her husband and her son. While she was in hiding with the Borst family they kept the back door locked, so that no unexpected visitors could just enter the house. Friends and neighbours found this a bit strange but Mrs Borst said it was because she was scared of the Germans, who were always on the lookout for young men who could be conscripted to work in Germany.

The Borst family home where Johanna was hidden (Picture: Jane Borst)

Luckily Willem Borst was in a reserved occupation as he worked on his father's farm. But the locked back door was important because Mrs Borst's brother and his wife were members of the NSB (the Dutch Nazis) and fanatically pro German. They lived in the same street, only a dozen houses from the Borst family, just a few minutes' walk away.

One evening when the back door had been left unlocked for some reason, Mrs Borst's brother turned up. Tante Jo was sitting at the sewing machine, and kept very calm and continued sewing. The lighting was subdued as they only had a few oil lamps. Mr

Borst mumbled that he didn't know anything about her, 'she is helping us with the sewing, because as you know my wife can't sew a stitch'.

Shortly after this Jane's aunt began to threaten the family: 'that woman is Jewish'. A neighbour too began to threaten.

It meant that this was the end of Jo's stay with the Borst family although at first Mr Borst did not think that it would amount to anything. However, Jo and Mrs Borst froze every time there was a knock at the door. So he was in contact with people in the underground to see if they could find a safer place for her. It did take some very anxious weeks to find a new safe place for Johanna to go into hiding

Jane Borst writes:

Sometime in late September two women from the underground network brought Tante Jo through the allotments at the back of our house to us. She lived in great anxiety with us, having to hide when we had any visitors. My mother was very anxious too as there were many Germans in Heemskerk, especially in the dunes.

Tante Jo had to stay indoors during the day. She was very handy with a sewing machine and made clothes for us children, as you could not buy anything in those days. Sometimes in the late evenings my mother and Tante Jo would go for a walk through the allotments towards the woods. Mother knew all the paths in the woods and so it was safe.

After a while my father heard from several people that some knew that we had a Jewish lady at home. Indeed we were sometimes threatened. My mother apparently said to my father that she didn't mind hiding a Jewish lady but couldn't he have found someone who didn't look so Jewish!

So a new hiding place had to be found for her.

The Borst family in Heemskerk:

Wilhelmus Borst (1912-1973),
Johanna Maria Borst-Offenberg (1908-2009),
Jane Borst (born 1938),
Willem Borst (born 1939).

The Pluis family in Beverwijk:

Mr and Mrs Pluis.
Daughters:
Christa and Sita.

The safe place that was found for my grandmother was with the Pluis family, who ran a milk and cheese shop in the Zeestraat in Beverwijk.

Christa is the elder daughter of the family and she was friendly with Riet, who was the sister of her future husband Jaap Poel. Riet Poel was a member of the same hockey club as Joop and Christa Poel is the daughter of the next family that hid her.

In June 2006 she wrote :

"I remember the day that 'Tante Jo' arrived, my sister Sita (14) and I (17) were already in bed when she arrived. She was brought to us by someone and she told us she was 'Tante Jo'. I can't remember much about the early time that she was with us

The Pluis family shop and home in Zeestraat, Beverwijk, is now a takeaway food shop. *(Picture: Google Maps)*

but it was just before Christmas 1942, and a lot of round-ups of Jews were being made.

"Mrs de Haan, who had brought her to us, came to get her then, because she lived nearby, because she had a hiding place underground, which we did not have. Your grandmother lay dead-still under the hall floorboards while the Germans were standing in the hallway.

"Later she said: 'I lay there next to a strange man, I ought to tell my husband!' She appeared apparently to be amused, but as a young girl I did not really understand what a sorrow she carried with her. I understood how her husband had been picked up on the other side of the street and how she had to keep on walking so as not to be betrayed.

"She also knew that her only son had tried to escape to England, but did not know if he had been successful. Maybe she talked to my mother about all this, because when it was dark in the evenings and you could still go out, they sometimes went out for a walk.

"Those first years nothing much shocking happened; my mother and father were busy with the shop – the fewer goods available the more burdensome it was; for example my father had to bicycle from Beverwijk to Zaandam to collect goods. Tante Jo did the housework, which during the war was no sinecure [a position requiring little or no work but giving the holder status or financial benefit]. When my sister came out of school and I came back from work, Tante Jo would bake oatmeal cookies in a small pan on the oil stove, which she cut into four equal parts so we would have something at tea time. My father didn't want any. He used to say: 'I don't like sweet things'. In the 'hunger winter' there was not a morsel of sweetness to be had."

[The Dutch famine of 1944–45, known as the Hongerwinter in Dutch [Hunger winter], was a famine that took place in the German-occupied part of the Netherlands, especially in the densely populated western provinces north of the great rivers.

South of the rivers had already been liberated by British and Canadian forces]

"A couple of times we received food from the Hoogovens [at IJmuiden, where Levie had worked as an electrician] for Tante Jo (once it was potatoes and red cabbage). Our contact was with the de Haan family, acquaintances of my parents and I believe a colleague of your grandfather's.

"Things were quiet until September 1944: the German occupation became stricter and food became scarcer. The highlight, however, was June 6, 1944 – the invasion of France and the war would soon be over! Alas the Germans became more nervous and decided the whole of IJmuiden and part of Velsen North should be evacuated, so that an eventual invasion there could be properly defended. All the employees of the blast furnaces had to remain and were housed in Beverwijk. The residents who did not work at the blast furnaces had to go away. So we too. My parents decided that we would go to Bussum, to one of my mother's sisters. We had an old baker's bicycle and three other bicycles available. We packed all that we could take with us and loaded it. The things that we were deeply attached to and could not be taken with us were hidden in the cellar. The cellar lid was barricaded with a large box.

"Then we were off, my father on the baker's bike and Tante Jo on the back of mother's bike. Alas, the baker's bike soon gave up the ghost when the wheels collapsed, and so with the three following bikes it was a question of walking. By chance we were overtaken by a horse and cart as we were walking along the canal towards Amsterdam, which was laden with evacuees from IJmuiden. Mum and Tante Jo got a ride as far as Sloterdijk near Amsterdam. One of the women on the cart asked my mother: 'isn't that Mrs Zwalf?', to which she replied: 'Oh no, that's my husband's cousin from Groningen'. The other woman did not say anything but she probably didn't believe it.

"In Sloterdijk we were to be accommodated in a school, but one of the organisers there said that as it was only for one night

we might as well sleep at his house and for Tante Jo a bed was available at a neighbour's house. The next day the neighbour said to Mum: 'I believe that last night I had a Jewish lady to stay'. Then we parted way, I went ahead with my father and later in the day my mother, Tante Jo and my sister followed on two bikes.

"Dad and I arrived in Bussum without any problems. The others arrived as well but after an anxious adventure. They were walking over the big bridge spanning the Amsterdam-Rhine canal when some people who were on bicycles under the bridge shouted something that they could not hear. But when they got to the top of the bridge they understood what was going on. At the other end of the bridge there were two German soldiers! They could not turn back as that would have aroused suspicion. So with Tante Jo on the back of the bike Mum got up speed going down the slope of the bridge and slipped through the middle of the two Krauts. So it went well!

"We stayed in Bussum for a fortnight. In the meantime, my father returned to Beverwijk and managed to arrange that we were allowed to return because, after all, shops were needed. Of the return journey I do not remember much. Food was scarce in Bussum and it was a long way to cycle with full panniers. When we got back everything seemed 'normal'. The shop had nearly nothing to be bought except with coupons and I was working at the gas company, which since November had no gas to deliver.

"In December there was another raid. Suddenly at home the lights went on and Tante Jo immediately said: 'There is a raid underway' and she was right. The building where the men who had been picked up (for compulsory work in Germany) were assembled had been connected to the electricity net and so the whole street was lit up. The two soldiers who came to our house found us standing in the hallway, my father with his marriage booklet in which it was noted that he had no sons only a wife and two daughters and the cleaner in the kitchen. One of the soldiers wanted to search the house, but the older one thought it all looked okay.

"That winter we spent by the wood burning stove and the oil lamp sticking food coupons, and we have never played a piano as much. It was on a Sunday in April 1945 (April 6) as we sat at table, we even had a small piece of meat, when the Tommies flew low over the house. We ran outside and waved and waved. All the neighbours were outside and so was Tante Jo. At last she could just go outside. The war was not officially over but for us it was. When we got inside again Tante Jo said: 'Even though we had meat today, who cares if it got cold!'. She always had a sense of humour and great strength of character.

"After the war there was a great shortage of housing in the Netherlands. Tante Jo lived with us until August 1945. Then she was allocated two rooms in a house with a family in the Cornelis Schuytstraat in Amsterdam, where she had use of a shared kitchen. She had only been there for a short while when she arrived completely upset at ours with a letter from the Red Cross. In her nervousness she had misunderstood the message. She understood that her husband was alive on August 10 but in fact the letter said that the Red Cross had received a message on August 10 that her husband had perished. She wept inconsolably. 'Had he been alive on August 10 he would have been here with me'. I don't know if by then she had had a message about your father but I think that she had.

"In November 1946 we bade her farewell when she left from Rotterdam for Melbourne. I don't know how long she stayed there but I do know that Jaap and I visited her and Tante Fre in the early 1950s one Saturday evening. The table had a beautiful tablecloth and lots of treats, which we were invited to help ourselves.

"It was very different to the Dutch polite restrictions: 'only one biscuit to one cup of tea'. It really was 'naschen', as she called it. [naschen in Yiddish means 'nose']. I also remember an occasion when I was walking between Tante Jo and Tante Fre and they said: 'It must be great to be that tall!', and indeed I did tower over them but they were two lovely little ladies, of whom I have many happy memories.

"When I married we moved to Ede, we kept in contact but less often. She did know that after a wait of eight years we had a son. Alas, not long after that she died."

J oop never spoke of his experiences. He only once told the story of his escape, and never mentioned any of his uncles, aunts or cousins who perished in the Holocaust – the exception was Tante Marianne and her children.

He was, however, close to some of his cousins. Lena and Jacob de Zoete were regular visitors to the family in Velsen. After the War he remained close to his cousins Hanna Gijlman-Zwalf and Bella Huisman-Mossel.

When we were in Holland we visited them quite a lot and we knew Frederika (Bella's mother) well as she and our grandmother lived together until 1960. We also knew Tante Jet (Hanna's mother) well.

Joop's uncles, aunts and cousins: *(cousins in CAPITALS)*:

On his mother's (Johanna) side: The Pampel family:

Jacob Pampel – Johanna's grandfather – (born 1854) married Bloeme Groen (born 1856): their children:

1. Abraham Pampel (1880-1944) married Vrouwtje Pels (1885-1960)

Lived and worked in Belgium, picked up on May 10, 1944 and transported on Transport 25 from Mechelen, Belgium on May 19. Arrived at Auschwitz on May 21, 1944 and immediately murdered.

Their sons:

JACOB PAMPEL, diamond polisher (1906-1942) married Lea Vos on January 3, 1933 and had a daughter Frieda (born August 20, 1934).

During a big raid at the end of August 1942 in Antwerp, the Pampel-Vos family was arrested and carried off to Mechelen. Jacob was sent to Northern France to be deployed there as forced labourer for the *Organization Todt*. His wife Lea and his daughter Frieda, however, were both deported to Auschwitz with the 8th Convoy, which departed from Mechelen on September 8 1942. The transport arrived in Auschwitz on September 10, 1942 and it is most likely that Lea Pampel-Vos, together with her daughter Frieda were murdered immediately on arrival at the gas chambers of Auschwitz-Birkenau. Jacob was deployed at the building of the 'Atlantic Wall' in Northern France but was added on October 21, 1942 to the 15th Convoy, together with another 237 'compulsory labourers', which left from Mechelen for Auschwitz on October 24, 1942. They arrived in Auschwitz on October 26 and it is presumed that he was immediately murdered.

MAX PAMPEL (1906-1993) survived and has descendants living in Belgium.

2.　Betje Pampel (November 23, 1882-September 24, 1943) married Salomon de Jong (November 9, 1882-October 22, 1943). Salomon was a Kaddish Cantor. Both deported to Auschwitz and murdered.

PHILIPPUS DE JONG January 29, 1911-Sobibor July 2, 1943. Butcher's assistant. Married to Hanna de Vries July 30, 1905-Sobibor July 2, 1943. Sales assistant. Possibly a child of this marriage survived.

JACOB DE JONG August 8, 1912-Auschwitz March 31, 1944. Laundry assistant.

MOSES DE JONG January 3, 1915-Auschwitz January 24, 1944 Shop assistant. His wife survived.

3.　Hartog Pampel (Sept 3, 1886-) Cigar and tobacco dealer in Alborg, Denmark. Married Elsa Christine Severine Schlamers (1886-?). Daughter **LYDIA PAMPEL** survived and had children Else and Henning Nielsen.

4. Hanna Pampel (August 25, 1888-Auschwitz September 21, 1942). Married to Elias de Zoete (January 7, 1882-Auschwitz September 21, 1942). Tailor.

LENA DE ZOETE (February 10, 1919-Auschwitz April 20, 1943). Married to David Mok (January 15, 1915-Mauthausen October 15, 1941). Merchant.

JACOB DE ZOETE (May 23, 1922-Sobibor July 2, 1943). Office clerk.

5. Johanna Pampel (October 10, 1890-February 28, 1962) married Levie Zwalf. Son Joseph, survived.
Children Willem and Christopher.

6. Marcus Pampel (May 27, 1893-Auschwitz January 31, 1943). Porter. Married Minet Emmerik (June 19, 1905-Auschwitz October 8, 1942).

Children: EMANUEL PAMPEL (August 15, 1924-Auschwitz September 30, 1942).

BLOEME PAMPEL (April 22, 1929-Auschwitz October 8, 1942).

7. Levie Pampel (July 29, 1895 -Auschwitz September 30, 1942) married Betje Roeper (June 29, 1895-Auschwitz August 19, 1942).

Children: JACOB PAMPEL (May 8, 1922-Sobibor June 4, 1943).

HENRI PAMPEL (June 26, 1933-Auschwitz August 19, 1942).

8. Frederika Pampel married Abraham Mossel (November 19, 1897-Middle Europe March 31, 1944). Fre and daughter BELLA survived. Two children: Philomena and Alfred.

Joop's father's family, the Zwalfs:

Joseph Zwalf – Joop's grandfather – (1841-1910) and his first wife Eva Godefroi had seven children, of whom only two survived to adulthood – Lea and Klara.

Moses 1871 (died shortly after birth), Hartog 1873 (died aged three), Mordechai 1875 (died at two weeks old), a stillborn boy 1876, Jacob 1878 (died at two days old) and:

1. Klara Zwalf (December 27, 1880-September 29, 1930). Unmarried.

2. Lea Zwalf (March 28, 1870-Sobibor March 23, 1943) married Soloman Boas (December 19, 1859-Auschwitz February 19, 1943). Probably no children.

Joseph Zwalf married Hanna Carels (June 16, 1855-June 26, 1936) the widow of Moses Salomon Salomons (a diamond cutter/polisher) in 1875, with whom she had five children: a stillborn girl in 1875 and stillborn boys 1876 and 1882.

Two surviving girls:

1. Grietje Salomons (November 26, 1877-Auschwitz February 5, 1943) married Louis Leyden van Amstel, market trader, (July 28, 1887-Auschwitz December 15, 1942).

Children: **SAMSON**, furrier, (March 24, 1919-Sobibor May 21, 1943) married Eva Alida Denneboom (April 6, 1916-Sobibor May 21, 1943).

HANNA (July 16, 1916-Sobibor May 28, 1943) married Jacob Courant, butcher, (August 11, 1917 –Sobibor May 28, 1943). Daughter Nanny Courant (September 1, 1940-Sobibor May 28, 1943).

2. Marianne Salomons (February 28, 1884-Sobibor May 28, 1943). Married her sister's brother-in-law Jacob Leyden van Amstel, market trader, musician, hairdresser (November 19, 1880-May 28, 1943)

MOZES, plumber (November 24, 1905-Hartheim September 3, 1941) married Rebecca Philips (January 24, 1908-Sobibor June 11, 1943). Children Marianne (November 8, 1933-Sobibor June 11, 1943), Heintje (March 29, 1935-Sobibor June 11, 1943).

ARON, lottery company sales representative (December 2, 1907-Auschwitz September 30, 1942) married Alida Muller (January 20, 1908-Auschwitz July 29, 1942). Son Jacob (March 14, 1936-Auschwitz July 29, 1942).

LOUIS, relief worker (July 12, 1910-Sobibor July 9, 1943) married to Esther Worms (August 21, 1902-Sobibor July 9, 1943). Daughter Marianne survived.

Joseph Zwalf and Hanna Carels had two children together:

1. Levie Zwalf (March 17, 1889-Auschwitz January 26, 1943) married Johanna Pampel (October 7, 1890-February 28, 1962).

Son Joseph (Joop) (September 19, 1918-April 6, 1982) escaped to England. Sons: Willem and Christopher.

2. Hartog Naphtali Zwalf (January 21, 1892-Sobibor July 2, 1943) married Jetta Barnstein (November 1, 1888-April 30, 1979). Daughter Hanna survived.

W hen on leave in Melbourne, Joop was occasionally required to accompany his commanding officer, Lt Gen Nico van Straten, to functions as his adjutant. [Nico van Straten had been decorated with the *Militaire Willems Orde* [Military Willems Order], the highest order for bravery in the Netherlands, the equivalent of the Victoria Cross.

He had been instrumental in destroying oil wells in the Netherlands East Indies and had held out on Timor, delaying the Japanese occupation of the island. With about 1,500 soldiers he held off a Japanese force of 2,000 men and delayed the occupation by 10 months.

On one such occasion at a formal dinner in a building called Coronado, Joop was seated at the far end of the table next to Patricia Mary Charlton, who had been working for the Australian Red Cross as part of the war effort, and who had only recently transferred to the Netherland East Indies Red Cross as an administrator. The rest, as they say, is history!

They married on July 8, 1943 at Christ Church, South Yarra, a church that had family connections for Patricia. During the first years of their marriage, Joop was regularly deployed in Dutch New Guinea.

At the end of the War Nico van Straten, who was the commanding officer of the Dutch Forces in Australia, asked Joop to help the Dutch Army to integrate those Dutch soldiers, like himself, who had married Australian women. At first this was under the auspices of the Dutch Army but by August 1945 the task was taken over by the Netherland Ministry of Foreign Affairs and Joop was employed as the resettlement officer in Melbourne at the Netherlands Consulate in Collins Street.

Soon his job changed from settling Dutch soldiers in Australia to the Dutch refugees from newly independent Indonesia. Some of these were Dutch citizens of Indonesian extraction but the official White Australia Policy meant they were not technically eligible to immigrate to Australia. He already had an 'arrangement' with an Australian immigration officer, whereby if he had Dutch citizens, who wanted to settle in Australia and who were part Indonesian and therefore ineligible to settle there, he would phone this officer and suggest that when he interviewed these prospective immigrants he should "close the curtains as it was such a sunny day"! This led to Joop being involved in the O'Keefe Affair.

In the meantime, Joop and Patricia's first son, Willem Anthony Louis (me!) was born in 1946 (Willem after Willem the Silent, Prince of Orange-Nassau, 1533-1584, who liberated the Netherlands from Spanish rule, and Louis after Joop's father). This was followed in 1949 by the birth of their second son Christopher Hendrik (Hendrik after Joop's uncle).

The O'Keefe Affair:

Samuel and Annie Jacob and their seven children had escaped the Japanese occupation of the Netherlands East Indies and had been put up in the Metropole Hotel in Melbourne, which they shared with the Netherland East Indies Army. Eventually they managed to rent the ground floor of a house in Melbourne (having been rejected by many landlords due to their colour) owned by retired postal clerk John O'Keefe.

Annie worked with the Dutch Red Cross (where Patricia worked) and Samuel was with the Netherland East Indies Intelligence service, as was Joop. In March 1944 Samuel was sent on an intelligence mission in Dutch New Guinea and asked John O'Keefe to look after his family if anything happened to him. Sadly Samuel died in a plane crash near Mossman. After the war the Australian Government tried to repatriate all non-European wartime evacuees. Some 800 wanted to stay permanently, including Annie Jacob and her children. As pressure increased for them to leave, in June 1947 Annie Jacob and John O'Keefe were married. However, the government maintained that the marriage did not give Annie the right to remain in Australia as a permanent resident.

Joop had been involved from the start of the affair, as the

file in the Australian National Archives attests. It was Joop who, according to the Australian Ministry of Immigration, had manipulated the whole affair.

According to the file it was Joop who in 1947 had asked if her 'exemption' to stay in Australia could be expedited as her children were still in education. By this time in March 1947 about 800 Indonesians had been repatriated and Joop had already intervened so that Mrs Jacob, as she still was then, should not be sent back.

The O'Keefe family in 1949.   *(Picture: paulbuddehistory.com)*

The file claims: "It is perfectly clear that Zwalf was taking very much a more than purely official interest in the case of Mrs Jacob, and it is possible that the date of the wedding to Mr O'Keefe was changed from June 21 to June 14 at his suggestion so that the Department of Immigration might be presented with a *fait accompli*. Zwalf was informed that Mrs O'Keefe's marriage would not confer on her any right to remain permanently in Australia."

In reply Zwalf stated that Mrs O'Keefe, formerly Mrs Jacob, lost her Netherlands nationality on her marriage and that she was no longer at liberty to enter The Netherlands or The Netherlands Indies. It appears that Zwalf had put the minister and the department in the invidious position of either deporting a woman who was now a British subject by marriage or to acquiesce in her remaining permanently in Australia'.

Despite this, in November 1947 arrangements were made for Mrs O'Keefe and her children to leave Australia by plane to the Netherlands Indies and an application was made to the consul for a visa. This was refused by the Dutch Government.

In early 1949 Immigration Minister Arthur Calwell issued a deportation order for Annie O'Keefe and her children. Joop again intervened by making a public statement concerning the O'Keefe family. This was picked up by most Australian newspapers, as well as newspapers in Indonesia and the Netherlands. Calwell's controversial deportation order and perceived lack of sympathy for the family attracted widespread criticism in Australia and overseas and captured the imagination of the media and the public, who rallied behind the O'Keefes.

The file continues: "It is clear beyond all reasonable doubt that Zwalf has shown throughout this affair a calculated and deliberate intention to aid and abet the O'Keefe family in their attempts to flout and circumvent the immigration and alien laws of the Commonwealth of Australia. He has far exceeded his duties as Secretary of the Consulate of a foreign government and that he should be regarded as a *persona non grata*. There were calls in the Australian Parliament for him to be expelled.

Through this entire affair the Dutch Government stood firmly behind Joop and backed up all he had done.

With financial assistance from public donations, the O'Keefe family appealed to the High Court of Australia, mounting what would become the first successful legal challenge to the Immigration Restriction Act 1901 (colloquially known as the White Australia Policy). This policy aimed to prevent the entry of non-European immigrants through the administration of a dictation test. In March 1949, the

High Court ruled that Annie O'Keefe could not be deported.

In 1953 Joop was called back to the Ministry of Foreign Affairs in The Hague and in October the family set sail on the Orient Line SS Orsova on its return maiden voyage to England. After arrival in London and sightseeing there, the family arrived in Amsterdam where his mother Johanna was living. After a few months stay in The Hague, Joop was posted as Netherlands Vice Consul in the Belgian Congo, also representing the Dutch Government in Portuguese Angola.

While in Leopoldville Joop and Patricia were active both in the Dutch and the ex-patriot community. They became very friendly with Patrick van Rensburg, who was the South African Vice Consul there. He was at first oblivious of the evils of the apartheid system but, through many long evenings in discussion with Joop and Patricia, came to realise how the apartheid system was unacceptable.

In his Book 'Guilty Land' Patrick van Rensburg refers to the fact that Joop and Patricia helped him to understand the evils of apartheid. He resigned as a protest against South Africa's apartheid policies of racial discrimination.

He joined the Liberal Party of South Africa, becoming the party's organising secretary for the Transvaal province in September 1958. In 1959 he moved to the UK, where he almost immediately began helping organise the 1960 campaign to boycott South African goods in the UK and the Netherlands.

Other organisers and supporters of the campaign included Julius Nyerere (later President of Tanzania), Bishop Trevor Huddleston, Canon John Collins and Tennyson Makiwane (assassinated in 1980). The Boycott Movement soon grew into the British Anti-Apartheid Movement. Van Rensburg was vilified by Afrikaners for his part in the campaign, and when he returned to South Africa in 1960, his passport was confiscated and he fled over the border to Swaziland. He settled in Botswana and founded a school and an independent newspaper there.

In February 1958 the family returned to The Hague and Joop was transferred as consul to Liège in Belgium.

While there, Joop decided that he should continue his studies, which had been interrupted in 1941 when Jews were no longer allowed to attend university. By this time he had developed an interest in law because much of his work in the consular department was concerned with the law. He enrolled as an external student at the University of Leiden and completed his degree and then his doctorate. His doctorate

Patrick van Rensburg's book.

was about international private law. The European Court of Human Rights quoted his doctorate in the case of inheritance in the Netherlands by an adopted child (adopted in the UK by a Dutch couple). At the time of adoption the Netherlands did not allow legal adoption but the ECHR declared that he was eligible to inherit based on the arguments in Joop's doctoral thesis.

While Joop and Patricia lived in Liege, Belgium, Wim and Chris were at school in Holland. Wim was in The Hague and Chris in Maastricht but then joined Wim in The Hague. In 1964 they both moved to England to boarding schools because it would become difficult, if not impossible, to further interrupt their education with their parents being posted to Canada. In Belgium it had been relatively easy as they both were only a train ride away from Liege and home. Up until then they had always been at home with Joop and Patricia.

In 1965 Joop was transferred to the Netherlands Embassy in Ottawa, Canada, as First Secretary for Economic Affairs. His seven years there included a lot of travel round Canada and reporting back to the Dutch Foreign Office on the nationalist upsurge of French Canada and its independence movement. He was also asked to report to the Dutch Parliament on the slaughter of baby seals in the Arctic (now Nunavut). In 1968 he spent three weeks in Inuit settlements in the far north Arctic reporting on the issue.

On April 30, 1969 (the Dutch *Koninginnedag* [the Queen's birthday, the Dutch national day]) the Dutch ambassador, on behalf of Queen Juliana, presented Joop with his award as Knight Officer of the Order of Oranje-Nassau. Joop had no idea that he was to be awarded this gong but Patricia had been told in confidence and so she made sure that both Christopher and I were at the National Day reception when he was presented with the insignia.

He was awarded his knighthood for his work in creating, with others, a union to represent diplomatic and consular staff of the Netherlands Foreign Office in negotiations over pay and conditions. His father, Louis, would have been extremely proud about Joop having been instrumental in the creation of a civil service union!

In 1971 Joop was asked to represent the Netherlands as Ambassador in Uruguay. This was considered a dangerous posting. For most of the 1900s, Uruguay was one of the most flourishing nations in Latin America. Uruguay's living standard nearly matched that of European industrialised nations with a complex social welfare system. During the Second World War Uruguay was considered the 'Switzerland of the Americas' as it made the majority of its profits through exporting agricultural goods, especially beef, but after the war food prices dropped in Europe and Asia, causing exports from Uruguay to decrease and resulting in lower wages for unionised workers, fewer social services, and increased national tension.

The *Tupamaros* [a Marxist-Leninist urban guerrilla group] formed in this time of instability, as a youthful group of students, trade union members and professionals. The movement began by staging bank robberies and businesses in the early 1960s, then distributing stolen food and money among the poor in Montevideo.

In June 1968, the President, Jorge Pacheco Areco, trying to suppress labour unrest, enforced a state of emergency and repealed all constitutional safeguards. The government imprisoned political dissidents, and brutally repressed demonstrations. The Tupamaro movement engaged then in political kidnappings, 'armed propaganda' and assassinations. Especially heinous was the kidnapping of the British ambassador to Uruguay, Geoffrey Jackson, who was held for nine months in a dark cellar, as well as the assassination of Dan Mitrione, a United States FBI agent who the Tupamaros learned was advising the Uruguayan police in torture and other security work.

The Tupamaros peaked as a guerrilla group in 1970 and 1971. During this period they made liberal use of their 'People's Prison' where they held those they kidnapped and interrogated them, before making the results of these interviews public. A number of these hostages were later ransomed for considerable sums of money, including the Brazilian Consul in Montevideo, Aloysio Dias Gomide. Their political violence since 1970 weakened its popular support. Also a wave of high-profile assassinations concentrated political opposition against them. By 1972 they were a much diminished group.

The background of the danger of the Tupermaros meant that Joop and Patricia were always accompanied by an armed bodyguard, provided by the Dutch Secret Service, and that the official residence and the embassy office were guarded by armed soldiers at all times. Despite these restrictions, they both enjoyed their time in Uruguay.

In 1976 Joop was recalled to The Hague to work at the Dutch Foreign Office, bringing his expertise in Private International Law to the task of bringing Dutch Private Law into line with Common Market Law (now the EU). His task was to re-write Dutch private law so that it was co-ordinated with the Common

Market directives. He enjoyed living back in the Netherlands – for the first time since 1942!

In 1979 Joop was made Consul General for the Netherlands in Houston, Texas. This post was of considerable importance to the Dutch Government as the Netherlands had extensive interest in oil and gas production and exploration. He retired from this posting in 1981 and he and Patricia settled in Baschurch, Shropshire, England. He had always said that he wanted to retire to England as it was the country that gave him refuge when he escaped the Holocaust by crossing the North Sea to be welcomed in the United Kingdom.

Joop died at home in Baschurch on April 6, 1982.

Joop's medals. From left: Knight Officer in the Order of Orange-Nassau, Bronze Cross, Victory Cross, Resistance Medal.

The House with the Double Shutters

Both Christopher and I were registered at birth with the surname Zwalf Leyden van Amstel. In itself this is a mouthful. Why Joop and Patricia registered us with this surname was always a mystery.

There was never a convincing reason given and in any case questions about the war were not welcome. However my research has shown that Joop's favourite aunts both married brothers whose surname was Leyden van Amstel. Perhaps it was an attempt to commemorate his aunts and his Leyden van Amstel cousins?

Another reason is, I believe, that the Leyden van Amstel name does not sound as Jewish as Zwalf. Certainly in the Netherlands it does not sound at all Jewish.

The only time Joop ever spoke about it was the somewhat cryptic remark that he did not want "to happen to you what happened to my family". This was long before we knew about the Zwalf family and the destruction of the Dutch Jews during the Second World War.

This story has been long in the making. I have been thinking about writing something for some years. As so much more information has come to light in the last few years, I have been spurred on by what I have learned from books, the internet and various family history societies.

However, I must give prominence to what I was told by my lovely grandmother and my father, even though what they told was fragmentary and sometimes withheld. Joop's favourite excuse was: "You can choose your friends, but God saddles you with your relatives!" I sometimes felt that this was a way of avoiding the question.

However, I must pay tribute to Jane Borst, whose family hid my grandmother and who has told me so much about that time, which, understandably, still haunts her.

Also to Christa Poel, whose family was the next to hide Johanna. She wrote to me a couple of times and then wrote a long letter with the details of Johanna's time with them, the Pluis family. From her previous letters I gathered that her story could be difficult to read and so it did take me few years before I could open the letter and read her story, which I have quoted, in translation, fully.

It was not until after my mother's death in 2001 that I found some photos of Joop in his pre-war years and also the letter from Henk Stol to my father telling of his visit to my grandfather in Westerbork. That too was hard to read.

Trudi Bos has written about the Jewish inhabitants of Velsen in her book: *Op zoek naar een plaats om thuis te komem* [Searching for a Place to Call Home]. She has done extensive research, especially about Louis' work at the Hoogovens and his membership of the Metal Workers Union. She has very generously allowed me use her work.

My thanks too must go to my cousin Max Zwalf, who unearthed the Parliamentary papers in the Australian National Archives about the O'Keefe Affair.

The Dutch National Institute for War Documentation and

Holocaust Studies and the Amsterdam Archives have been extremely helpful going back to the 1980s when I started on this quest. They have always been prompt in replying and have given me much help in interpreting some of my findings.

I have written this really for my children – Luke, Hannah and Leah – and for my niece Liesbeth and nephews Tristan, Sebastian and Oliver, in the hope that this story will not be forgotten and that their great-grandparents, Louis and Johanna, and their grandparents, Joop and Patricia, may live on at least through these pages.

My gratitude also goes to Steve Penny, who has edited this for me and has made many very useful suggestions and also directed me to other source material. I could never have completed this without his help.

Above all, my thanks go to my wife Helen, who has been very patient with my family history hobby over many years, particularly while I have been writing this book.

Any mistakes I have made in writing it are all my own.

Wim Zwalf,
November 2024

The House with the Double Shutters

Bos T – Op zoek naar een plaats om thuis te komen
(Stichting Uitgeverij Noord Holland)

Bredero B – De Grote Oversteek
(Montero Curacao)

Bruin J and van der Werff J – Vrijheid achter de Horizon
(van Reemst)

Cooke P and Shepherd B H eds – European Resistance in the
Second World War (Pen and Sword Praetorian Press)

De Lange L – Het verhaal van mijn leven (Uitgeverij van Oorschot)

De Vries A J, et al – Een stevige pleister op mijn neus
(Historische Kring Heemskerk)

Dessing A – Tulpen voor Wilhemina (Bert Bakker)

Frank A – Het Achterhuis. Dagboekbrieven
14 Juni 1942-1 Augustus 1944 (Contact Publishing)

Gilbert M – Atlas of the Holocaust (Routledge)

Gilbert M – The Holocaust (Collins)

Greenman L – An Englishman in Auschwitz
(Vallentine Mitchell in the Library of Holocaust Testimonies)

Klempner M – The heart has reasons (Pilgrim Press)

Kuper S – Ajax, the Dutch, the War (Bold Type Books)

Moore B – Victims and Survivors – the Nazi Persecution of
the Jews in the Netherlands 1940-1945 (Arnold)

Nortier JJ – Acties in de Archipel (Wever)

Olsen L – Last Hope Island (Scribe)

Presser J – Ashes in the Wind –the Destruction of Dutch Jewry
(Souvenir Press)

Rees L – Auschwitz (BBC Books)

Sprenger J ed – Gezichten van Joods Verzet
(Nederlandse Kring voor Joodse Genealogie)

Vincent A and Bosman AJ – Een gemeente in oorlogstijd:
Velsen 1940-45 (Historische Kring Velsen 1995)

Visser F – De Schakel (Forum Boekerij)

Printed in Dunstable, United Kingdom

66946446R00067